W9-CIF-856

It's Not *Just*
About the Ribbons

Also by Jane Savoie

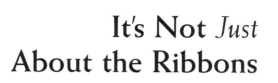

It's Not *Just*
About the Ribbons

It's About Enriching Riding and Life
with Innovative Tools and Winning Strategies

Illustrations by
Beth Preston

Foreword by
Sally Swift

Trafalgar Square Publishing
North Pomfret, Vermont

First published in 2003 by
Trafalgar Square Publishing
North Pomfret, Vermont 05053

Printed in Hong Kong

Library of Congress Cataloging-in-Publication Data

Savoie, Jane.
    It's not just about the ribbons : it's about enriching riding and life with innovative
tools and winning strategies / by Jane Savoie.
        p. cm.
Includes bibliographical references and index.
    ISBN 1-57076-255-4 (hardcover)
1. Horsemanship—Psychological aspects. I. Title.
SF309 .S318 2003
798.2'01'9—dc21

                                    2003010654

Book design by Carrie Fradkin
Typeface: Weidemann, Rotis Sans Serif, Rotis Sans

10 9 8 7 6 5 4 3 2 1

Contents

Dedication

Dedicated with love to Rene and Myrtle Savoie—my favorite father- and mother-in-law. You're the best!

Acknowledgments

I want to thank all my cheerleaders for their unwavering support and encouragement throughout the process of creating this book. I couldn't have done it without you.

Thank you also to:

My husband, Rhett, who has always been the wind beneath my wings.

Both my families: David and Lorraine Kaplan, and all the Savoies.

Caroline Robbins, who wears many hats as my publisher, editor, advisor, and, most importantly, friend.

Martha Cook, managing editor at Trafalgar Square Publishing, for her quiet efficiency and enormously valuable input.

Beth Preston for her incredibly brilliant illustrations.

Lynn Palm and Marcia Kulak for being so generous with their time while answering my questions about Western riding and jumping.

To all my wonderful students and friends for always being there. I appreciate your enthusiastic pompom waving more than you'll ever know. And, to all of you who have invited me to speak and allowed me to share my message at your events—I'm honored.

Foreword

In *It's Not Just About the Ribbons,* Jane Savoie has done it again. After a lot of research, she has produced a second dandy book about her favorite subject—using mental training to enhance riding, and life in general. It is an important sequel to That Winning Feeling!

This new book expands on some of the wonderful ideas she gave us in the first book, and adds to them with new questions to answer and new ways of answering them. She presents new images and explains why they are successful. She introduces many new ideas and techniques, and adds actual real-life accounts of problems that have been solved with the sensible use of her procedures and strategies. She makes it all look so easy that you realize with a little self-discipline you can do the same thing!

The book moves along in logical sequence. Each chapter covers specific tools for improvement using information from earlier chapters and building on the foundation established. Jane never lets you feel lost in a sea of details; sometimes, she uses material that will be discussed in a future chapter, but she always makes it known so you constantly have a feeling for the whole, which keeps expanding as you read. She frequently intersperses her text with real, often fascinating examples of riders she knows, and how they and their horses have benefited from the techniques she is presenting. This makes the book even more interesting and potent.

As you may know, I have a special interest in the use of visualization and use of the mind in all disciplines of riding. Jane has packed this book full of such information and more, and made it very easy to digest. It's a very satisfying and stimulating read.

Sally Swift
Author of *Centered Riding* and *Centered Riding 2: Further Exploration*

How to Use This Book

Why a Second Book?

In 1992, after several years of studying the work of peak-performance experts to help me deal with my "mental monsters," I wrote my first book, *That Winning Feeling! Program Your Mind for Peak Performance*. The sports psychology tools and techniques I described had been a lifeline for me during the four years I was making my bid for a spot on the 1992 U. S. Olympic dressage team destined to go to Barcelona. By writing the book, I hoped that the ideas that had helped me through those difficult times could be useful to other riders—not only to improve their skills, but also to help them better enjoy the time they spent with their horses.

I was delighted that readers in all riding disciplines found the concepts helpful. It was even more exciting to me that many of them figured out how to take those ideas and apply them to other areas of their lives such as career goals, personal relationships, financial aspirations, and even challenges like dealing with a life-threatening illness, or the loss of a loved one.

My research didn't stop when *That Winning Feeling!* was published. All I had to do was look back over my own personal growth to be convinced of the value of this sports psychology stuff. I had gone from being an insecure, nervous competitor filled with all kinds of self-doubt and fears, to a confident and calm contender. I remember one of the other short-listed riders, Hilda Gurney, saying to me at the final selection trials in Orlando, Florida that I was the only one of the twelve riders who looked as if she was having a good time. My response was that I was having a *terrific* time! Thanks to all my mental training and preparation, I was able to really relax and savor the entire experience.

My own transformation was enough to get me hooked on mental training. I found that in a very basic way, mental training is similar to learning how to ride. That is, in both my riding and my personal growth, I am constantly searching, learning, changing, and growing. My education comes in stages much like peeling away the layers of an onion. The more I learn about striving for excellence in every area of my life, the more I find there is to know about this fascinating field of human development.

My primary motive for writing a second book is to share with you some of what I've learned since my first book was published. In addition, this new book is an answer to the many requests I've received from readers of *That Winning Feeling!* who embraced that book and are hungry for more information. Those people just aren't willing to settle. They are eager to set a higher standard, make some changes, and become the kind of riders they've always dreamed of being.

So what will you find in this book? At the beginning, you'll recognize that some of the material is a review of the information covered in *That Winning Feeling!* Bear with me as I feel it's important to revisit those basic ideas because in this book, I'll be expanding and delving deeper into the use of tools and concepts such as *goals and motivation*; the *power of the subconscious mind*; *visualization*; *self-talk*; the *"As If" Principle;* and the *importance of attitude*.

You'll also find lots of new material that will take you a little deeper into mental training. I do this by introducing new techniques and ideas such as:

Modeling top riders

Asking better questions

Neuro-associative conditioning and creating verbal and physical anchors

Changing your physiology

Role-playing

The brain-wave/emotion connection

Getting an attitude adjustment

Sonic meditation

Belly breathing

Changing your "mental software" with affirmations
Using buzzwords
Diluting the negative
Developing an attitude of gratitude
Stepping out of the comfort zone into the achievement zone
Having a fire in the belly
Building concentration muscles
Bargaining with fear

These tools, and many more, will help you improve your actual riding skills as well as your overall enjoyment of your sport. The best part is, you'll find you can make changes much more easily and playfully than you can when you're limited by the standard approach of using just willpower or iron-jawed determination to get results.

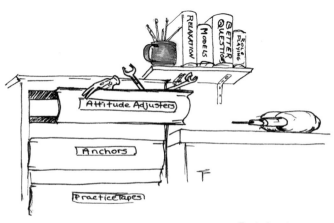

Tools for change

I learned firsthand that change doesn't have to be effortful. In the past, I had always been the kind of person who thought that as long as I was disciplined and determined, I could achieve my goals. In many areas of my life, that was true. But, when it came to my riding, no matter how hard I tried, I was still plagued with chronic position problems such as sitting crookedly, and I still struggled with emotional issues like being easily distracted and very nervous in competition.

Because the traditional approach just wasn't working for me, I started my research to learn better ways to overcome my riding challenges. I discovered that "drilling" and willpower were not the only—or even the best—answers, and that there are many other ways to create change. What follows in this book is the result of almost two decades of research into those alternative methods.

Since your emotions and personality traits rule your world, I will also show you how to create changes in them so you can reach your best—both in your riding and in your life.

I differentiate between *emotions* and *personality traits* because I don't think they are exactly the same. Emotions are all about the way you feel at a given moment in time. You might not experience a negative emotion such as being frustrated, angry, sullen, discouraged, or afraid all of the time. But when you do, emotions like these can really prevent you from enjoying your riding.

Traits, on the other hand, are characteristics that dominate your personality, and they pretty much determine how you handle situations. For instance, if you are the type of person who deals with life's challenges by being unsympathetic, insecure, impatient, anxious, full of self-doubt, arrogant, pessimistic, or unfocused, you'll have a profoundly negative effect not only on yourself but on your horse.

Since our emotions and traits determine our behavior, wouldn't you love to have the ability to change the way you feel and act quickly and easily? After all, if we want to improve, we *have* to make some changes. And we're more apt to follow through with a program if the process is relatively easy.

So, if you had a wish list, which are some of the bad emotions you'd like to change, and which emotions might serve you better? Maybe you'd like to turn *anger* into *emotional detachment*, *moodiness* into *evenly tempered*, *discouragement* into *resilience*, or *fear* into *courage*.

How about those negative personality traits that are holding you back? Which traits would make you a better rider and your horse a happier animal? How would you like to be able to turn *lacking empathy* into *being sympathetic, insecurity* into *confidence*, *impatience* into *patience*, *tension* into *relaxation*, *self-doubt* into *belief*, *arrogance* into *humility*, *pessimism* into *optimism*, or even the tendency to get *distracted* into unshakable *concentration*?

This certainly sounds like a lot to tackle. Since I don't want you to be overwhelmed by a long discussion of all negative emotions or personality traits at once, I'm going to deal with one at a time. So, between each main chapter, I will concentrate briefly on a single emotion or trait that causes difficulty and give you case histories of people who either embody the opposing *positive* emotion or trait, or tell you about people who have successfully enacted change from bad to good. The only exception will be my discussion on turning *fear* into *courage*. This is such a pervasive and crippling emotion for riders that, at the end of the book, I devote an entire chapter to it.

At the end of each chapter, I'll summarize the key points I've discussed under the heading *"Essentials,"* so you'll have them for easy reference. And, at the end of each section on an emotion or trait, I'll highlight the main concepts under *"Tips for Change."*

As you read about the different tools and techniques for creating change, you'll find that some of these solutions will work for you and that some will work better for others. It is my hope that by the end of the book you have lots of options to choose from and you can simply tailor your personal development program to fit your specific needs.

I'm now going to begin our quest for creating change by discussing *goals,* and how important motivation is for reaching those goals. After all, in order to change and improve, you not only have to know what you're aiming for, but you also have to be intensely motivated to make those changes. Otherwise, you'll just stay in your *comfort zone* and settle for less than you deserve. (See *Comfort Zone*, p. 50.)

Define Your Destination

Goal Setting

In order to reach your personal best in any area of your life, you need to set definite, long-term goals so that you know exactly where you're heading. Think of how futile it would be for you to get into your car to go to a horse show but not know where it is or how to get there! How can you arrive someplace if you don't know where you're going?

Goal setting is the key to any success plan because when you *define your destination*, you create the future in advance. It doesn't matter whether you're a recreational rider or an Olympic hopeful, you need goals—not only to give you something con-  crete to work toward, but also to help you measure your progress along the way.

If you don't know where you're going, you won't know when you get there.

So, what kind of goals are you going to set? I personally believe that if you're going to have a goal, you might as well make it a big one. Big goals are exciting, and that excitement keeps you on track when the going gets rough. I understand that setting a big goal may be a daunting prospect, but I encourage you to dream a little. Live life with the philosophy that it's better to try to do something and fail, than try to do nothing and succeed.

As I said in *That Winning Feeling!* make sure, however, to make a distinction between big goals and unrealistic goals. A big, exciting goal should be just out of reach but not out of sight. It encourages you to stretch yourself but is not so far-fetched that, in your heart, you consider it unattainable.[1]

When your destination is unrealistic and seems unreachable, the goal-setting process can backfire. In fact, you are actually more apt to give up before you even get out of your driveway because you'll have a "what's the use" attitude. For example, it's ridiculous to set your sights on competing as a member of next year's Olympic Three-Day Event team when neither you nor your horse has ever competed above Training Level. That kind of unrealistic goal sets you up for discouragement and failure. Instead, choose a big but obtainable destination such as making your debut at Preliminary Level by the end of the competitive season.

Why Goals Work

Part of the reason why *defining your destination* works is because you eventually experience whatever you consistently focus on. As you think, so you create.[2]

Another reason why *defining your destination* works is that once you define what you want and your brain acknowledges you don't have it, you become dissatisfied. That dissatisfaction creates internal pressure. You can take advantage of this pressure by letting it prompt you to take action.

So put a little pressure on yourself. Tell your friends about your goals. Make your goals known to someone who inspires you, like your instructor. Since you won't want to disappoint someone you respect, you'll be more apt to follow through with your plans. You can also put some pressure on yourself by putting your goals on a piece of paper and reading them aloud to yourself every single day.[3] You'll feel uncomfortable if you haven't done anything to move yourself toward your goal, and that feeling alone should motivate you to take some action.

The Road Map

It's important to have destinations that excite you, but, if you focus entirely on the end results, you're bound to feel anxious and occasionally frustrated. That's because you're not always the one in control of end-result goals. You're not necessarily the one who decides who wins a class, is chosen for a team, or gets a particular score.

Short-Term Goals

To avoid getting frustrated, break your end-result goals down into manageable, short-term goals. These short-term goals not only allow you to measure your progress but they also serve as *motivational reinforcements* (see *Motivation*, p. 14). Think of them as places on the *road map* that tell you that you're on the right route and that you're getting close to your destination. As you achieve each short-term goal, you'll be encouraged to proceed to the next step. Remember, it's the journey as much as the destination. Enjoy the scenery along the way!

Think of your short-term goals as places on a road map, telling you that you're on the right route.

Focusing on where you are on your *road map* rather than on your final destination also reduces anxiety. Rather than having an end-result goal of scoring sixty-five percent in a dressage test or placing in the top three in an equitation class, make a new goal that reflects your effort rather than the outcome. Your new goal can be something like sitting elegantly and quietly, maintaining a metronome-like rhythm, or staying totally focused throughout an entire ride, class, test, pattern, or course.

Break your short-term goals down into daily, weekly, or monthly objectives. When you look at your *road map*, it should be clear to you how your route brings you—step-by-step—closer to your ultimate destination. If it isn't, you need to make a new map by adjusting, resetting, or restating your short-term goals.

Let's say your long-term goal is to compete in a 100-mile endurance ride. You know it'll take three seasons for you to successfully condition your horse so that he can complete the competition in good shape. As you start your first season, your personal *road map* might look something like this:

Your *Daily* Goals

1. Do your *mental rehearsal* and *affirmations* (see p. 72 and p. 97).
2. Eat a nutritious diet to keep as fit as possible.
3. Read at least 15 minutes each day to continue to learn about subjects such as nutrition; conditioning your horse; mental training for competition; dressage to increase your communication and improve your horse's athletic ability; and proper cooling down techniques.
4. During today's ride, work on keeping hands quiet. Practice trot-canter-trot transitions.

Your *Weekly* Goals

1. Take one dressage lesson to learn more about bending and suppling exercises, engagement of the hindquarters, and improving communication.
2. Get videotaped to review lessons and study these rides on non-lesson days.
3. Get longed at least once a week to work on your position.
4. Ride when it's rainy, windy, or very hot to practice coping in conditions that are less than ideal.
5. Improve personal fitness by doing aerobic exercise (walking, jogging, cycling, dancing, rowing) three times a week and strength training two to three times per week.

Your Horse's *Weekly* Goals

1. Start with six to eight weeks of long slow distance work to build a solid foundation of fitness. Alternate walking and trotting for five or six miles (about one hour) within the horse's heart rate of 100–140 bpm (beats per minute) on an every-other-day schedule.
2. Gradually, increase the demands by slowly increasing the mileage until the total working distance is no more than thirty miles per week.
3. Carefully, add intensity by doing more trotting or adding some slow canter work, for 1 to 5 minutes at a time.
4. Elevate horse's heart rate to 170 bpm briefly, by adding in some easy hills.

5. After the initial conditioning, do workouts based on a two-week cycle. Do five workouts in a two-week period. Do four hour-long exercise periods at an average of 10 mph. Keep the horse's heart rate between 110–150 bpm. Elevate heart rate to 170 bpm briefly with an occasional gallop. Your fifth workout should be a longer ride at a slower speed. Start the longer, slower ride at less than 10 mph for a distance of ten miles, and over two months increase the distance to 18 miles.

6. Incorporate two more dressage sessions on days between conditioning work.

7. On one of the dressage days, do some "gymnastics" such as cavaletti work or jumping grids.[4]

The Language of Goal-Setting

When you *define your destination*, be sure to use very precise language. Three of the most common mistakes people make when setting goals are misstating them by making them *vague*; saying them in a *negative* way; or stating them in the *future* tense.

An example of a vague goal is to say, "I want to be a better rider." Instead, say, "I sit straight and centered," "I give subtle but effective aids," or "I have an independent seat."

Another ill-defined goal is to say something like, "I want to move my horse up a level." Be specific. Give yourself a deadline. "At the Fox Hollow Horse Trials on May 14, my horse and I have our debut at Preliminary Level."

Secondly, when setting goals, make sure you state them in a positive way. You sabotage yourself if you use negative words such as, "I *won't* stiffen when I ride a shoulder-in," or, "I will *not* get nervous at shows," or, "I *don't* get distracted by what other riders do."

The reason negative language backfires is because there's no picture in your mind for the word "not." Therefore, your brain simply perceives "stiffen," "nervous," and "distracted" as your goals. It only registers, "I stiffen when I ride shoulder-in," or, "I will get nervous at shows," or, "I do get distracted by what other riders do." Replace the negatively phrased goals with positive ones such as, "When I ride shoulder-in, I *am* supple and loose," "I *am* calm and relaxed in competition," or, "I *stay* totally focused when I ride."

You sabotage yourself if you state goals negatively.

Finally, be sure to state your goals in the present tense *as if* you've already arrived at your destination. In Chapter 5, I explain how your mind always moves you toward what you focus on—toward your current *dominant thought.* That's why it's important to imagine your destination *as if* you've already reached it. (More on the *"As If" Principle* later in this chapter.) It's not enough to replace, "I won't be nervous at shows" with "I will be relaxed at shows." You need to say, "I AM relaxed at shows."[5]

The following is an excerpt from a letter I received from a young rider. This girl learned a valuable lesson about the importance of "languaging" her goals in a positive way and in the present tense. She writes:

"My name is Susan and I am twelve years old. I own and event a 14.2 hand Quarter Horse pony. Last fall, I moved up from the Beginner Novice level to the Novice level, and I started to have some problems. My pony would take advantage of me and stop at any jump she could. It was awful, and it made me very upset. Those problems (or "challenges," as you would call them) continued throughout the fall season and started back in the spring. One evening after a Pony Club eventing rally, one of my friends told me about your audiotape, *That Winning Feeling!* She tried to describe it, but couldn't, so the next day she let me borrow the tape. That night I listened and figured out my problem. I was not telling my mind what I really wanted. I had been repeating, "I will not have any refusals" in my head, which was really programming myself to have refusals. So that night I began repeating in my head, "I go clear," and, sure enough, the next few events, I did go clear!"

To get you started on the right track, here are some examples of how to reword your goals like Susan did so that they are precise, positive, and in the present tense.

Poorly Phrased Goals	Well-Constructed Goals
I won't get stressed in competition.	I am calm and relaxed in competition.
I will not be distracted by physical discomfort.	I easily block out physical discomfort.
I will not be influenced by what I see other riders do in warm-up.	I stay focused and stick to my own plan when warming up.
I won't lose my focus because of all the chaos at the show.	I stay in my own cocoon of concentration at the show.
My horse does not flip out when he has to leave the other horses.	My horse is secure and always on the aids.
I don't get exhausted.	I'm incredibly fit and strong.
I am not panicked by drop jumps.	I love jumping drops!
I do not find my balance in my horse's mouth.	I have a balanced and independent seat.
My goal is to not try so hard.	I let things flow.
I'll do fabulous sliding stops.	I do fabulous sliding stops.
I won't let triple combinations freak me out.	Triple combinations are my favorite jumps.

Write Your Destination Down

It's not enough to *define your destination* in your head. You need to write it down. There is an almost magical power in the written word. When you *define your destination* by writing it down, you really begin to design your future.

Word your goals carefully, and then put them down on paper. I write mine on three-by-five-inch index cards. I place these cards where I'll see them often, such as on the visor in my car, in my tack trunk, and on my refrigerator door. Look at your file cards often. Claim your destination out loud (even if only to yourself) several times a day.

You can even write out a goal contract like the one that follows as a symbol of your commitment.

Goal Contract

Date: _____

Starting immediately, my goal is to develop an independent seat.
I do this by:
1. Getting myself worked on the longe line.
2. Studying tapes of beautiful riders.
3. Visualizing myself giving quiet aids from an elegant and beautiful position.
4. Riding without stirrups.
I am one hundred percent committed to reaching my destination.
This is a binding contract that I make with myself.
Signed:_____

As you look at your goal contract, make it more powerful by using the power of *visualization*. I go into the specifics of visualization in Chapters 7, 13, and 19, but for now, create a vivid image of having already reached your destination by filling in the following details:

What are you wearing?

What does your horse look like?

Where are you riding?

Punch up the images by involving your senses:

☞ Hear the rhythm of your horse's footfalls.

☞ Smell the clean, fresh air after a late afternoon thunderstorm.

☞ See yourself sitting perfectly centered and in harmony with your horse.

☞ Feel an elastic contact with his mouth.

Get Motivated

Fill Your Gas Tank

Suppose I ask you to drive my car from Philadelphia to Miami. I give you the entire weekend to organize your trip. You can use that time to pack your clothes,

stock your cooler with snacks and drinks, buy a map, and plan your route. On Monday morning, you get in the car and start your journey. Sound easy? There's only one catch. There's no gas in the tank. And without fuel, you're left stuck in the driveway.

Just as you need gas in your car to start your journey, you also need to *fill your gas tank* before you can pursue your goal. *Motivation* is your fuel. Like the "Energizer Bunny," motivation gets you started and keeps you going—in spite of the inevitable setbacks that occur while riding and training. Having an empty gas tank is as defeating for you as it is for your car. In fact, a lack of motivation is probably the biggest challenge standing in the way of achieving any of your goals—including improving your riding.

Once you decide on your destination, *fill your gas tank* by doing two things. First, figure out *the reasons why* your goal is important to you. Second, learn how to *link less pain and more pleasure* to pursuing this goal. I'll discuss both of these concepts next.

The Reasons Why

If you know why your goal is important to you, you'll remain motivated by reminding yourself of *the reasons why* you chose that destination in the first place. *The reasons why* you want to get somewhere come first. The answers as to how you're going to get there come second.

So ask yourself why you chose a specific goal. Why do you want to qualify for the finals? Why do you want to win one of those silver belt buckles? Why do you want to move up to a higher level of competition? Why do you want an independent seat? Why do you want to be less timid, angry, frustrated, or insecure? Why do you want to excel in your discipline? What are *the reasons why* you are committed to doing whatever it takes to arrive at your destination?

Write down a list of all *the reasons why* and keep them handy. If they're written down on paper, you'll have them for quick reference when you feel your motivation flagging.[6]

The Carrot or the Stick

The second way to *fill your gas tank* is *to link less pain and more pleasure* to going after your goal by using a concept I call *the carrot or the stick.* In a nutshell, *the carrot or the stick* assumes that all motivation actually boils down to two needs—the need to seek pleasure and the need to avoid pain. The way we do anything—getting to work on time, studying for an exam, buying a bouquet of flowers for someone we care about—is motivated by gaining pleasure or avoiding pain.

However, we often have mixed emotions because certain situations bring us both pleasure and pain, and in these cases, we nearly always do more to avoid pain—*the stick*—than we will to gain pleasure—*the carrot.* The only situation when pleasure is a stronger motivator than pain is when the potential for pleasure *far* outweighs the potential for pain.[7]

Take my desire, for example, to quit smoking. At the age of twenty-four, I had already been a smoker for nine years. At the time I wanted to quit, I was up to three packs a day. Having a cigarette was on my mind every minute. I knew I'd have a lot of pain if I tried to quit. I'd have to deal with constant craving as I struggled to break this habit. But, I also associated a lot of advantages to quitting. I would be beating an addiction that controlled me. I'd be making my husband very happy. I'd be able to breathe a lot better. (Here I was trying to be an athlete, and I was getting winded walking up three flights of stairs!) I'd save quite a bit of money. My

Most of us will do more to avoid pain than to gain pleasure.

clothes, hair and breath wouldn't smell like an ashtray. I wouldn't annoy the non-smokers that I hung out with. Fortunately, all the pleasure I could gain from quitting far outweighed the pain of going through "detox." So, I managed to stop smoking, and haven't had any desire for a cigarette in the thirty years since.

CASE HISTORIES

Joanne and Linda

In most cases, however, *the stick* is the stronger motivator. To illustrate this, I want to tell you about two girls, Joanne and Linda.

Joanne, a talented rider, isn't very motivated. She comes up with all sorts of reasons to blow off her daily schooling session or her weekly lesson with me. If she manages to get herself to the barn, more often than not, she ends up hacking her horse instead of working him. That's fine if her goal is to be a recreational rider who rides occasionally for fun. But, she claims her goal is to train her horse so that eventually she can compete at the Grand Prix level in dressage. She "talks the talk," but she definitely doesn't "walk the walk"!

I tell Joanne that I can provide her with all the information and tools she needs to learn how to ride the Grand Prix. The one thing I can't give her, no matter how hard I try, is motivation. The best intentions in the world aren't going to do her any good if she continues making excuses and avoids doing the work.

Let's see if we can figure out why Joanne isn't totally committed to her goal. To understand why she is so unmotivated, we need to figure out how her behavior allows her to gain pleasure and avoid pain.

Look at it from two angles by asking yourself the following questions. What pleasure and pain does she get from committing herself to her goal to compete at Grand Prix? Also, what pleasure and pain does she get from *not* going after her goal? On the one hand, committing herself to her goal and going after it with conviction could bring her lots of pleasure in the form of awards, recognition from peers, fun, improved self-esteem, and greater confidence in her ability.

On the other hand, striving to attain her goal could potentially create pain in the form of hard work, discipline, and fear of not being good enough, looking foolish, or being embarrassed.

What pleasure does Joanne associate from *not* going after her goal wholeheartedly? She gets a chance to relax and recharge her batteries. She has more time to have fun with her friends. She feels an overwhelming sense of relief because she has taken the pressure off herself. With the pressure gone, she can now stay in her *comfort zone*—the place where she feels totally safe and never threatened or challenged.

What pain does she associate with *not* going after her goal? She loses the opportunity to compete at Grand Prix—a huge accomplishment. She loses face with her peers. She's bored because she isn't challenging herself.

There's potential for both pleasure and pain in this situation. That fact, in itself, puts her in conflict. But, remember what I said earlier. The need to avoid pain is almost always greater than the need to gain pleasure. Joanne ultimately doesn't commit herself to her goal because the need to avoid the pain of the work, of not being good enough, and possibly being embarrassed if she doesn't do well, is far stronger than the need to gain pleasure from her accomplishment.

Linda's story is another example of how *the carrot or the stick* function as motivators. She was trying out for a place on the U.S. Three-Day Event team to compete at the World Championships, and her actions were influenced by the same need to avoid pain that dictated Joanne's behavior.

Linda has been a student of mine for over twenty years. She is a very gifted rider. She is a kind and empathetic person who has the ability to develop all different types of horses so that they happily reach their potential. In the early 1990's, Linda started campaigning three different horses and was enormously successful with all of them. At the beginning of the competitive season, she placed in the top three at every event she entered. However, once she was at the top of the list to be picked for the team, she started to feel very uncomfortable. To reduce her discomfort, she deliberately, but unconsciously, sabotaged herself so that she didn't place well in her next few events.

I'll tell you how we actually dealt with Linda's self-sabotage right after this chapter ends when I look at the personality trait, *insecurity*. But for now, let's figure out what motivated her to do this to herself. To do so we have to look at how much pleasure and pain, respectively, she associated with winning.

She would potentially get shortlisted for the team with *all* of her horses, providing her comfort in knowing that she would have a sound horse on the day of the big event. She would get a lot of recognition, and her picture would be in all the magazines. The owners of her horses would be pleased, which would make her job more secure. She'd be one step closer to wearing her country's flag on her saddle pad at an international event.

With all this pleasure associated with winning, the pain had to pretty intense in order for Linda to sabotage herself. Just what was the pain that she linked to success? I believe it boiled down to two things—pressure and insecurity.

First of all, by winning she'd feel pressure, not only from herself, but also from her horse's owners and from the public to maintain the standard she had reached. The pressure to keep up that level of performance was overwhelming.

Second, as talented as she was, she had a real issue with confidence. We all know how confidence is essential to our ability to ride well. Most people would agree that no matter how skilled or talented you are, if your confidence level is low, you won't do very well. (See *Insecurity,* p. 21.) Well, Linda was incredibly insecure. She just didn't possess an unshakable belief in her abilities and she had put a ceiling on what she thought she was capable of achieving. So, when she ended up doing well at several events, she was way out of her *comfort zone*. The feeling, "It's not like me to do so well all the time," "This is a fluke," and, "I'll never be able to keep this up," made her very anxious.

The pain from all the internal and external pressures plus her insecurity and self-doubt were so much more powerful than all the pleasure Linda could derive from winning. And since, as I told you, we nearly always do more to avoid pain than we do to gain pleasure, Linda "choked" so she could take the pressure off herself. Once she got back into her *comfort zone*, which she did by losing some competitions, she felt she could start competing wholeheartedly again.

Essentials of Goal Setting and Motivation

- *Define your destination.* Set long-term goals so you know where you're heading.
- *Make a road map.* Break long-term goals into manageable short-term goals that serve as motivational reinforcements and let you measure your progress.
- *Word your goals thoughtfully.* When you word them, be sure to make them precise, state them in a positive way, and say them in the present tense.
- Commit yourself to your goals by writing them down.
- *Know the reasons why.* Once you *define your destination*, write down all *the reasons why* that goal is important to you. Knowing why your goal is important will help keep you motivated.
- *The carrot or the stick* is the basis for all motivation. The carrot is our need to gain pleasure. The stick is our basic human need to avoid pain. If your motivation is flagging, you need to *link more pleasure and less pain* to the pursuit of your goals.

2

Insecurity

I think most people suffer from insecurity or lack of confidence to one degree or another. It's an extremely common trait that the majority of us struggle with throughout our lives. But I also think that riders, as a group, suffer from insecurity more so than other people. Maybe this is because our horses continually humble us, we constantly struggle to master new skills, we hit plateaus in training, and we compare ourselves to others and find that we always come up short.

Insecurity can cause all kinds of problems. For instance, you may find it difficult to ride confidently unless you are getting constant feedback from another person. Though, if you're fortunate enough to always ride under supervision, you could become dependent on your trainer and not think for yourself or trust your own judgment. If, like most of us, you ride on your own much of the time, you probably second-guess yourself. Insecurity makes you torture yourself with questions like:

"Am I ruining my horse?"

"Am I screwing up?"

"Do I look like an idiot?"

"Do people think I'm a terrible rider?"

"Do people think my horse looks awful?"

"Will I ever get this right?"

"Why can't I just do this better?"

(I'll discuss how to *ask a better question* in Chapter 17, pp. 151 and 156.)

I know from personal experience that insecurity can undermine your efforts and make you miserable. Even when it appeared that I was achieving a great deal of success with my horses, deep down inside, I didn't think I measured up. I remember my reaction when the shortlist of twelve riders for the Barcelona Olympics was first released. I read the list over and could understand why the other eleven riders deserved to be on it. After all, they were all wonderful, gifted, experienced trainers. But in my mind I thought, "What am I doing on this list? I don't belong in that company. I wonder when the selection committee will realize they've made a mistake."

To truly enjoy yourself, you need to be able to turn insecurity into confidence. Let's return to Linda whose story I started on page 18, and follow her progress in her bid for a slot on a World Championship Three-Day Event team. You'll see how her insecurity affected her and what she did to overcome it.

Remember that early in the season, Linda had been doing spectacularly well. She won or placed in every single event she entered. Unfortunately, winning all the time made her very uncomfortable. She was so insecure that she believed that much of her success was due to dumb luck, and there was only one way to go in the placings, and that was down. Linda reasoned that it was only a matter of time before she blew it. So in order to get back into her *comfort zone*, she deliberately, but unconsciously, sabotaged herself at her next few events to take some of the pressure off. Once that was done, she felt she could attack again.

The reality is that Linda didn't need to sabotage herself. She's an extraordinary rider who is well-prepared, and so are her horses. There really isn't any reason that on any given day, she shouldn't come out at, or near the top. But your internal thermostat doesn't listen to reason or logic. It reacts to your *self-image*, whether that image is accurate or not. (See *Self-Image*, p. 50.) Linda's insecure self-image said, "I'm not that good. I'm not experienced enough. I don't deserve to do this well. The professionals should be winning these events." A self-image like this will cause you to sabotage your own happiness by consciously or subconsciously finding logical reasons why you can't possibly succeed. Then, you proceed to act in a way that supports these reasons.[1]

Linda and I discussed her self-sabotage. I asked her if she really worked so hard, invested so much time, energy, effort, and money into her riding and then, on the day of the competition, put her horses on the trailer, got in her truck, drove down the driveway saying, "I hope I lose today!" She giggled at that picture. Intellectually, she understood what I was saying, but her insecurity was stronger than her logic.

Linda's self-image needed to be changed. She had to believe in herself and see herself as perfectly capable of being a tough, consistent, formidable competitor. We started by reprogramming her subconscious mind with mental pictures of her feeling confident, secure, and most importantly, deserving of her success as she picked up her winning ribbon (See *Visualization*, Chs. 7, 13 and 19). We also programmed her subconscious mind with *self-talk* such as, "I'm well-prepared and I deserve to be on top," and, "My horses are great horses." (See *Self-Talk*, Chs. 11 and 17.) Linda liked this exercise but we didn't stop there. I helped her bust through her self-imposed limiting beliefs by explaining to her how to train fleas! (See *beliefs*, p. 107.)

The Jumping Flea

I learned about training fleas from Zig Ziglar in his book, *See You at the Top*.[2] The process is really quite simple. I'll walk you through it here.

First, get a glass container like a peanut butter or mayonnaise jar. Make sure you clean it out well or things can get messy.

Next, find your neighborhood dog and "borrow" a bunch of fleas from him. Put the fleas in the jar and just observe them for a while. You'll notice that they jump around very enthusiastically. Before you know it, they jump right out of the jar.

Then go and find another dog and get some more fleas. Put the new fleas in the jar, but this time, place the lid on top. These fleas will also start to jump around. As they do, they hit their heads on the cover of the jar.

Now, fleas are not stupid. This new batch of fleas will soon realize that if they jump just a bit shy of the lid, they won't hit their heads and get little flea headaches and concussions. When you see this happen, take the lid off the jar. And can you guess what they do? You got it! The fleas don't jump out of the jar! The lid is off and they're perfectly capable of jumping out, but they don't even try because they *think* that they can't.

I explained to Linda that this is what she was doing to herself. She had placed

Don't be like the flea that's been trained to limit its own potential.

a lid on her abilities. She didn't believe she could "jump out of the jar," although she was certainly capable of doing so. She had arbitrarily put a ceiling on her ability, and she could just as easily choose to remove it. Her perception of her limits wasn't real; it existed only in her mind. So every time she felt her old insecurities creep back in, I reminded her to be a *jumping flea*, and "break through the ceiling." As she busted through her old limiting beliefs, she experienced a lot of success. As a result, her self-image eventually evolved from one of insecurity to one of confidence.

By the way, Linda made the Three-Day Event team on two of her horses. She rode one as a team member and the other as an individual and placed extremely well with both of them. What about you? Wouldn't you love to leave your insecurities behind and become a confident, self-assured rider?

Here are two more tools for turning insecurity into confidence. They are the *"As If" Principle* , and *Changing Your Physiology.*

The "As If" Principle

In *That Winning Feeling!* I explained that by acting *as if* you possess a certain emotion, eventually you'll feel that way for real.

Part of the reason that acting *as if* is just as effective as actually feeling a positive emotion is that, as far as your physiology is concerned, the chemistry of *faked* emotion is identical to the chemistry of *real* emotion.[3] In fact, if you are hooked up to machines that measure biological functions such as brain-wave activity and heart rate, you'll see that the readings on these machines are the same when you're pretending to feel an emotion as they are when you're actually experiencing this emotion.

So, if you want to be confident, act *as if* you're confident. It doesn't matter whether you actually feel this way or not. Pretend that you're self-assured and brimming with confidence, and eventually you will be.

Denny Emerson, member of the Three-Day team that won the gold medal at the 1974 World Championships, long-time eventer, and trainer of many successful horses and riders, agrees that acting *as if* you possess a quality or emotion is an important part of the process of making it happen. Denny calls it "practicing traits." He explains, "People seem to understand the power of practice when it comes to

skills. You know you'll get better if you practice a riding skill like a shoulder-in or a right-lead canter transition. Well, you can also practice *traits.* You can practice *courage.* You can practice *self-confidence.* You can practice *optimism.* You can practice things that you might not think are able to be practiced, such as being a better friend to yourself or not always denigrating yourself."

If you struggle with assuming a positive emotion, do some *role-playing.* Act *as if* you're a rider you really admire. Since you are no longer you, you can go beyond your self-imposed limits and become a *jumping flea* who escapes from the jar! (See *Role-Playing*, p. 112).

If you think you don't know how to mimic the physiology of confidence, think of a rider who is the epitome of confidence and act *as if* you're her.[4] Take Lynn Palm, for example. Lynn is a four-time winner of the American Quarter Horse

Lynn Palm on
My Royal Lark
(left) and Larks
Joint Account

Association's *World Champion Superhorse* title. She tells me she never gets nervous at shows. She absolutely can't wait to get into the ring. As she makes her entrance with Royal Lark, she sits up straight yet relaxed, with shoulders back, eyes up, and a self-assured expression on her face. She absolutely exudes poise and confidence.

Change Your Physiology

Remember the age-old question about which comes first, the chicken or the egg? Well, you can ask the same about your emotions and your physiology. That is, do you change the way you feel by changing your physiology, or do you change your physiology by changing your emotions? To say it another way, do you sing because you're happy or are you happy because you sing? Unlike the chicken-and-the-egg dilemma, however, there is an answer to this question: *action precedes emotion*— you don't *get* feelings, you *do* feelings. You don't *get* insecure (or depressed, frustrated, or angry), you *do* insecurity (or depression, frustration, or anger).

You *do* each of these emotions with a very specific physiology. Research shows that there is a definite link between the movement of facial muscles and distinct emotional responses such as anger, fear, disgust, and happiness. It stands to reason then, that since you *do* emotions with your physiology, you have a choice. If you want to transform your emotions, do something different with your physiology. A *tiny* change in how you use your body, face, and voice instantly alters how you feel. This is called *changing your physiology.* For example, think about how you breathe and use your voice, face, and body when you're feeling insecure. Then, change the way you feel on the inside by projecting confidence on the outside.

Let's test how *changing your physiology* works. Try the following experiment. No matter how you're feeling right now, act as if you're confident and self-assured. Move around energetically with your eyes up, shoulders back, and a huge smile on your face. Then laugh out loud. Speak with authority. While you're doing all that, try to feel insecure. Pretty difficult, isn't it?

Now allow the corners of your mouth to drop. Shuffle around slowly as if you're exhausted. Make sure you slump your shoulders. Look down at the ground shyly rather than making eye contact with anyone. Speak slowly, softly, and haltingly. When you adopt that physiology on the outside, don't you find it very difficult to feel full of confidence on the inside?[5]

Faces in the Jar

When I want to project a particular emotion on the outside, I sometimes think about the Beatles' song, *Eleanor Rigby*: she "waits at the window wearing the face that she keeps in the jar by the door." I have lots of faces in my jar. I put one on depending on how I need to feel in any given situation. If I'm

Choose your face depending on how you want to feel

tired, but I have to teach four more riding lessons, I pull out an energetic and enthusiastic face. If I have to give a lecture to a large group, I pull out the face of relaxation and confidence. If I have to compete at a big show, I pull out the face of poise and concentration.

What faces do you keep in your jar? What faces would help you truly enjoy your riding? Is it the face of confidence? The face of patience? Or, perhaps you need to wear the face of courage.

Now you know how to set goals, get and stay motivated, destroy limiting beliefs, assume winning qualities by acting *as if*, and transform your emotions by *changing your physiology*. In the next chapter, I'll show you how to create lasting change through a technique called *Neuro-Associative Conditioning (NAC)*. ☼

Insecurity to Confidence

TIPS FOR CHANGE

- If you want to become more confident, you have to change your *self-image*.

- The only limits you have are the ones you put on yourself. Be a *jumping flea* and bust through old, limiting beliefs.

- To become more confident, use *visualization* and *self-talk* to reprogram your subconscious mind.

- Use the *"As If" Principle* to turn insecurity into confidence. It works because the chemistry of *faked* emotion is identical to the chemistry of *real* emotion.

- The way you look on the outside has a direct effect on the way you feel on the inside. To change the way you feel, *change your physiology*. Move, breathe, talk, and act *as if* you're confident.

- If you don't know how to mimic the physiology of confidence, do some *role-playing*. Pick a rider who embodies the trait you want and act *as if* you're her.

3

Neuro-Associative Conditioning

Now you have *set some goals* and *filled your gas tank* so you're motivated to do whatever it takes to reach your destination. But when you go to ride your horse, reality sets in.

No matter how hard you may try, you still struggle with your emotions. You become frightened if your horse is overly fresh. You get angry and impatient when your horse just doesn't "get it." You lose your resolve to ride when the weather is lousy or you're tired. You get frustrated when you just can't seem to master a new skill or movement. You get tense and distracted at shows, and you get discouraged when you place near the bottom of a class.

You might ask if there's anything else you can do to change the way you feel so that you ride better and enjoy yourself more? The answer is a resounding "yes." It involves an excellent technique called *Neuro-Associative Conditioning (NAC)*.

I learned about *NAC* from Anthony Robbins, "personal-power" coach, and author of *Awaken the Giant Within*. The heart of *NAC* is a simple three-step process to create lasting change by changing your emotional programming. Through this process, you can change an emotion, a feeling, and even a behavior. Just for fun, I'm going to call this process *Getting the NAC.*

Getting the NAC

Understanding what motivates you is the first step to changing your behavior while the next is to actually change your conditioning. I'll briefly describe

Robbins' three fundamentals to create lasting change, and later on, I'll give you some case histories to illustrate them.

Step 1. *Create leverage*. Remember *the carrot or the stick* from the last chapter? You'll use this concept of pleasure and pain as motivators to inspire yourself to change.

First, determine the pain and the pleasure you associate with behavior change. Then, think about how much it hurts if you *don't* change and how if you *do* change, you'll gain pleasure. To do this, link negative consequences like embarrassment, ridicule, frustration, or depression to your current actions and positive consequences like pride, increased self-esteem, confidence, or exhilaration to desired actions.

Let me give you a quick story to illustrate this point. Let's say you're twenty-five pounds overweight. You've known for a while that you should lose weight, but you *really* get a lot of pleasure from eating as much as you want—especially sweets. One day, however, you take a good look in the mirror and think, "That's it! I've had enough! I hate looking like this!" You decide it hurts too much to endure how you look, how you feel so uncomfortable in clothes that are too tight, and how you have such poor self-esteem and low energy. Once you reach a point when all that pain outweighs the pleasure of indulging your appetite, you have the *leverage* you need to do something about your weight.

Step 2. Do a *pattern interrupt*. This important step breaks your current, limiting pattern of association. Jolt yourself by doing something unexpected or totally outrageous so that you interrupt whatever you're doing or feeling at the moment. Make a rapid movement like jumping up and down or spinning around, shout out something silly or inappropriate, or whistle a happy tune.

To get back to my example of being overweight, when you feel like reaching for a big slice of chocolate cake, do a *pattern interrupt* by yelling

Interrupt negative thinking by sticking your thumbs in your ears and wiggling your fingers.

"Stop!" at the top of your lungs or sticking your thumbs in your ears and wiggling your fingers. That'll probably make you laugh out loud which, in itself, is a good *pattern interrupt*.

Step 3. *Recondition* and *reinforce*. The third and final step of *NAC* is to *recondition*—that is, create a new association by linking tremendous pleasure to a new, better behavior, and *reinforce* that association until it becomes conditioned.[1]

Again, imagine turning down that piece of chocolate cake. Focus on all the pleasure you get from being so disciplined and in control. Savor a sense of accomplishment. Feel proud of yourself for having the resolve to stick to your new, healthful way of eating. See yourself holding your head up high as you walk into a party feeling totally comfortable with how you look. Reinforce this association by repeating it over and over again until it becomes conditioned.

CASE HISTORIES

Here are a few stories about riders who learned to *Get the NAC*. The first is Jennifer, who needed to overcome her anxiety and dread about riding in a clinic. The next two are people who overcame negative emotions like embarrassment and fear. Finally, I'll tell about how I used *Getting the NAC* on my dog, Emma.

Jennifer

Here's the scenario. A famous coach was coming to our area for the weekend to teach a clinic. Jennifer wanted to ride with him, but she dragged her feet about signing up because she had mixed emotions about attending. It was *a carrot or stick* situation.

The *"carrots"* were:

☛ She would get an objective evaluation of her horse's past training from a world-renowned trainer.

☛ Benefit from new information and tools for training her horse.

☛ Spend some "quality" time with her horse.

☛ Have a chance to learn new techniques by watching the coach with other horses and riders.

☛ Have an opportunity to grow by taking herself out of her *comfort zone.*

☛ Her horse would get exposure to a new situation.

☛ The people who were watching would see how far her horse had progressed, so she'd get a lot of positive reinforcement from her peers.

The *"sticks"* were:

☛ She would worry that the trainer would hate her horse.

☛ Concern that her horse would be pushed too hard, and he'd have a meltdown.

- Be too nervous to ride in front of a lot of spectators.
- Be embarrassed if she didn't ride well that day.
- Her ex-trainer would be at the clinic, and she didn't want to run into her.
- Be anxious because her horse didn't travel well and would be unsettled when he got to a new place.
- The cost of the clinic, stabling, and two nights at a hotel would strain her budget.

Jennifer was torn because she associated equal amounts of pleasure and pain with riding in the clinic. And, as you already know, the *stick* is a stronger motivator than the *carrot*, so she ultimately decided to stay home. She justified her decision by telling her friends that her horse had only just been back in work a month after a lay-up, and he wasn't fit enough yet. In her heart, Jennifer knew that she really should go because there were so many benefits to be had by riding in it. I told her there was a solution to her dilemma. By *Getting the NAC* she could actually change her feelings about participating.

1. I explained to Jennifer how to *create leverage.* She did this by counting the negative aspects of not riding in the clinic.

She would:
- Lose a tremendous educational experience.
- Miss out on a chance to do something really fun with her horse.
- Pass up an opportunity to expose her horse to new experiences.
- Feel angry and disgusted with herself for chickening out, and, as a result her self-esteem would plummet.
- Make it much more difficult to face the next challenge that came along because she didn't confront her fear this time.

2. I described how to do a *pattern interrupt.* As soon as Jennifer found herself thinking that she'd be better off staying at home, she did something bizarre like jump up and down as fast as she could for thirty seconds, or yell out, "Yahoo!!!!!" at the top of her lungs.

3. Finally, once she'd broken her pattern, I told her how she could *recondition* herself by linking new, intensely pleasurable associations to riding in the clinic. Then, I had her *reinforce* these new associations by repeating them until they became conditioned.

They included:

- ☞ Feeling a huge sense of accomplishment as she imagined mastering a new exercise.
- ☞ Reveling in being strong and adventurous.
- ☞ Savoring how proud she was of her horse.
- ☞ Indulging in a sense of satisfactory accomplishment because she'd brought her horse to his current level of training.
- ☞ Imagining how gratified she would be when the instructor complimented her on her riding and her horse.
- ☞ "Seeing" her name and photo published in a magazine or newsletter as a participant in the clinic.
- ☞ Experiencing how rewarding it was when her horse trusted her enough to concentrate in a new, scary arena because she'd taken the time to build a partnership.
- ☞ By repeating these new associations often and intensely, Jennifer *reconditioned* and *reinforced* them so that she soon enthusiastically looked forward to riding in the clinic.

Eileen and Mary

There are two very common emotions that riders experience—embarrassment and fear. I'm first going to describe how Eileen and Mary figured out the pleasure and the pain associated with these feelings, and then I'll demonstrate how they created lasting change for themselves by going through the three steps of *NAC*.

EMBARRASSMENT

Eileen had taken her hunter, Blackjack, to some horse shows and had consistently done poorly. She was so mortified by her performance that her brain linked the pain of embarrassment with being at a competition. Since she couldn't face dealing with this pain, she stopped competing altogether. In fact, she so completely linked pain with competing, every time she even picked up an entry form, she felt ill.

Eileen had decided to stop competing, but she wasn't entirely comfortable with this choice because she felt guilty about being such a wimp and knew there was much to gain from experiences in the show ring. Her task was to change her feelings about showing, and she used *NAC* to do just that. Here's what Eileen did.

First, she *created leverage*. She decided why she absolutely *must* change. To do this, she figured out why *not* changing would cause her more pain than changing: If she didn't show, she'd sacrifice having fun with friends, outings with her horse, experiences in the show ring, and getting important feedback from a fresh eye.

Next, she did a *pattern interrupt*. She interrupted her current unpleasant association with competing by doing something surprising. She picked a show and scanned through the classes she could enter. As soon as she started to feel anxious, she broke this "pattern" in order to "scramble" her brain. Sometimes, she stood up and spun around three times. Other times, she just shouted out loud, "Quit it!"

Finally, Eileen *reconditioned* and *reinforced*: She followed up her *pattern interrupt* by creating an empowering alternative to embarrassment, and *reinforced* it until it became *conditioned.* She thought of a time in her life when she had felt a great sense of accomplishment. Eileen remembered how proud she was when she had found the discipline and determination necessary to train and get fit enough to compete in a 10K race. She relived the pleasure of this feeling, and as she filled out an entry form, she conjured up that memory—she felt herself being strong, proud, and in control.

Spin around to interrupt your negative train of thought.

Then, Eileen amplified those feelings by several notches. She "heard" people congratulate her, made colors more vivid and the sounds around her louder and happier. She also became more associated with her feelings; she didn't watch herself in a dissociated way as if she was on a movie screen, but became fully associated by seeing herself *in* the picture as if she was looking from the inside out. She repeated this new association over and over until she linked new, pleasurable emotions to competing.

FEAR

Mary had a fear of being longed on her horse. (I'll be covering the subject of *fear* in great detail in Chapter 21, but, for now, here's a look at how Mary *Got the NAC.*)

One day, while taking a longe lesson to work on her position, Mary lost her balance and slipped off her horse. Trying to break her fall with her hand, she broke her wrist. This accident caused Mary to link physical pain with being longed. She refused to get on the longe line because the memory of her accident was so intense that she just didn't want to risk going through it again.

As with the other riders I've told you about, deep down inside, she knew how valuable those longe lessons were and how much they could help her riding. Mary knew she had to change her feelings and behavior she associated with getting longed. The way to do this was to reprogram herself and attach feelings of pleasure to longe lessons.

Mary *created leverage* by asking herself, "Why *must* I change?" If she didn't take longe lessons, she'd miss out on an opportunity to improve her seat and make it more independent. Also, even more compelling, was the realization that her horse would be happier and more comfortable if she could stop pulling on his mouth to find her balance.

So, when Mary panicked at the thought of being longed, she did a *pattern interrupt*: In her mind, she pictured herself on the longe line doing exercises. As soon as the fear surfaced and she started to tighten up, she snapped an elastic band she wore around her wrist. Ow! That interrupted her pattern, for sure!

Mary followed-up her *pattern interrupt* by *reconditioning* and *reinforcing* herself with a new association. She thought of a time when she felt courageous, bold, adventurous, or free-spirited. Sometimes, it was during a particularly good lesson. Other times, it was on a lively hack with friends. Occasionally, it was at a horse show. She remembered how much fun and how empowering it was to feel that way. She experienced those emotions deeply again, and as she did, she "saw" herself on the longe line. She repeated these images until she linked feelings of bravery and fun to the idea of being longed.

Emma sitting in front of the fridge

Emma

Keep in mind that *Getting the NAC* isn't confined to your work with your horses. You can use it in all areas of your life. You might remember my dog, Emma, from the cover of the paperback edition of *That Winning Feeling!* I realize that this situation doesn't fit neatly into the three steps of *NAC* because, after all, a dog, can't *create leverage* for herself. Nonetheless, it's an amusing story about how I used the basic principles of *NAC* to *recondition* Emma so that she actually came to enjoy taking her pills.

Emma is getting on in years and needs daily medication to keep her from having "accidents" in the house. After a while, she became convinced that taking this medicine was a painful experience. I tried, unsuccessfully, to hide the pill in any number of treats like peanut butter, a piece of a hot dog, or a spoonful of canned dog food. She always managed to eat the treat and spit out the pill. Since Emma had to take her medicine three times a day, this process was an ordeal for both of us, and soon created enough leverage for me to want to make a change.

So, I had the *leverage,* but before I could *recondition* Emma so she'd associate pleasure with taking her medicine, I had to do a *pattern interrupt.* Each day when it was "time," I'd pick up the vial of pills. As soon as she saw me do this, she'd start to slink off in the opposite direction. I did an outrageous *pattern interrupt* by dancing around and singing, "It's yummy medicine time!" to the tune of the old "Howdy Doody" theme song. This, I'm sure, was quite a sight. But, Emma thought it was fun, and rather than trying to escape when she saw me reach for the pills, she'd join in the excitement of the song and dance.

Once I had broken Emma's pattern, I *reconditioned* her by linking a source of pleasure to her medicine. I'd put the pill in the back of her throat and then go to the refrigerator and give her a piece of cheese. Doing this so often on a daily basis helped to *reinforce* this new association.

Emma now so completely links pleasure with taking her medicine. As soon as I start singing the "yummy medicine" song, she gets up from wherever she is, walks eagerly over to the refrigerator, and sits in front of it!

Anchors

Now I'm going to introduce you to *anchors.* You *anchor* the new, pleasurable feelings you created when you *reconditioned* and *reinforced* in Step 3 of *Getting the NAC* with a key word, phrase, or action. By doing so, you can conjure up these feelings on cue while you're actually riding.

An *anchor* is a learned association between a specific emotional state and a specific trigger. The *anchor* can be either *verbal* or *physical.*

We always *anchor* things in our minds. Whenever we're in a highly emotional state, we link whatever we're consistently experiencing at that moment to that state.[2] For example, if every time you compete you feel exhilarated, you probably link increased levels of pleasure to showing. On the other hand, if you feel sick to your stomach, you most likely link pain to showing.

In the three case histories you've just read about anxiety, embarrassment, and fear, the riders might well have used *verbal anchors*. You say these *verbal anchors* out loud during Step 3 of *Getting the NAC* when you *recondition* and *reinforce*. I call these words *"buzzwords."* Good examples of *buzzwords* are: "strong," "capable," "adventurous," "bold," "determined," and "powerful." Once you've *anchored* your new, empowering feelings with a *buzzword*, you can simply use this word when actually faced with doing something that makes you uncomfortable. (See *Buzzwords*, p. 101.)

You can also use a *physical* cue as an *anchor*. For example, there is a useful relaxation exercise called *clicking the pen.* To do this exercise, first make a tight fist and increase the tension in your hand. Second, let go of the tension by uncurling your fingers and "see" the word "relax" written on your palm. Third, say the word "relax" and touch your thumb and forefinger together. The unique action of touching your thumb to your forefinger while you're relaxed, *anchors* a feeling of relaxation with that *physical* cue. Then, whenever you feel tense while riding, all you have to do is touch your thumb to your forefinger, and a feeling of relaxation should wash over you. (More on *clicking the pen* on p. 89.)

You can even customize your own specific *verbal* or *physical anchor* to help you with bad habits that have crept into your riding position. What is it that you habitually do that you'd like to change? Do you collapse one side of your body? Do you pull on one rein all of the time? Does your lower leg move around too much? Do your muscles get tense when you do lateral work?

CASE HISTORY

Christine

I helped one of my students, Christine, use a *verbal anchor* to deal with her position problem. Christine had a real challenge with her seat and right leg. The problem started because she collapsed her right hip and her seat shifted over to the left side of the horse. She then drew her right leg up so that it looked about three inch-

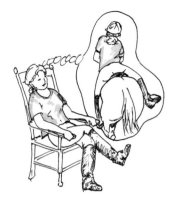

Christine started changing her position when she wasn't riding by picturing her unbalanced seat.

She broke her negative pattern by jumping up and down and shouting in "Chinese."

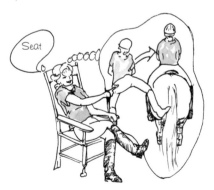

Then, she changed her position in her mind and anchored the correction by saying, "Seat."

es shorter than her left leg. She had the *leverage* necessary to change this bad habit because she knew that when she wasn't centered, she made it difficult for her horse to balance himself.

We began by changing Christine's position when she wasn't riding. She pictured herself sitting off to the left with her right leg drawn up. She made the image very vivid by filling in details. She saw what she was wearing, she smelled the freshly mown grass beside the ring, she felt the weight of the reins in her hands, and she heard the rhythm of the footfalls of her horse's trot.

Christine experienced this scene fully in her mind, and then she broke her pattern by jumping up and down while she spoke as fast as she could in Chinese. (By the way, she doesn't speak Chinese. She just pretended.) It was an outrageous *pattern interrupt*! She then *reconditioned* by picturing moving her left seat bone toward the center of the saddle. From her newly balanced position, she was able to stretch her right leg down. I had her *reinforce* this adjustment by repeating it in her mind many times.

Each time Christine made the correction in her mind, she *anchored* it to a *buzzword* by saying the word "seat." She did this so many times that now all she has to do when she rides and feels herself sitting crookedly and drawing her right leg up is say "seat." This *buzzword* triggers her to center her body and stretch her right leg down.

Essentials of Neuro-Associative Conditioning

- If you want to make permanent changes in a behavior, emotion, feeling, or riding habit, you need to *Get the NAC.* It is a three-step process:

    1. *Create leverage.* Decide why you *must* change.
    2. Do a *pattern interrupt.* Break your current pattern or association by doing something outrageous.
    3. *Recondition* and *reinforce.* Create a new association and *reinforce* it until it becomes conditioned.

- Create verbal or physical anchors so you can quickly and easily conjure up your new emotion or behavior.

4

Frustration

Frustration is often seen in riders. We all have a lot invested in our horses in terms of effort, energy, emotion, and money, and, we tend to be perfectionists. When we don't measure up to our own often unrealistic standards, we get frustrated with ourselves.

Riding is more frustrating than many other sports because you're not only dealing with your own, sometimes uncooperative body, but you also have to deal with the character, mood, and physical limitations of another living being. Although it's perfectly normal to get frustrated when you're struggling, it can create many problems:

1. Foremost, frustration is counterproductive to good riding and training. When you get frustrated, you automatically get tense. Rarely can you make any progress when you're in this kind of emotional and physical state.

2. You're going to transmit your feelings to your horse and he's going to become frustrated as well.

3. If you don't do something to dissolve frustration, it can escalate into anger. A rider tends to take her anger out on her horse by becoming overly aggressive and punishing him harshly for even the smallest evasion or resistance. This is hardly the type of training atmosphere conducive to producing a willing partner.

If you find yourself often getting frustrated, you need to have some tools to help you let go of this destructive emotion. I use any one of a number of relaxation exercises to dissipate frustration and the tension that comes with it. One of the most practical techniques is to take a short walk on a loose rein and do what I call the *sleeping dog*. You'll find a description of this *belly-breathing* exercise and other simple relaxation exercises in Chapter 9.

Celebrate Little Victories

Celebrate the small victories.

You can also defuse frustration by giving yourself an *attitude adjustment*. (See Chapter 15, *Attitude is Everything*.) One way I've learned how to do this is to train myself to *celebrate little victories* and accomplishments both in riding and with my horse.

As far as my own riding is concerned, I've learned not to beat myself up if I'm not perfect. Sometimes, I have to look pretty hard to find something to celebrate. Often, it's something as simple as being pleased that I've controlled my upper body, kept my hands quiet, stayed supple in my wrists, or concentrated better.

I also celebrate every small accomplishment with my horse. I'm thrilled when I can add just a little bit more bend to my lateral work. I'm happy when he stays in front of my leg. I get excited that he tries so hard to do what I ask, even if we aren't completely successful.

Stay Emotionally Detached

Regardless of your mount's antics, sit quietly, and don't take his behavior personally.

Another way I've learned to give myself an *attitude adjustment* is to *stay emotionally detached*. This allows me to be less intense about training and, therefore, I enjoy the process a whole lot more. I've used two techniques to help me stay relaxed and keep those less-than-stellar rides in perspective.

I learned how to adjust my attitude toward my horse while watching Kyra Kyrklund, Finland's premier dressage star, at the United States Dressage Federation's training symposium in Scottsdale, Arizona in 1998. Kyra rode several of the horses there. Sometimes, through tension, confusion, or willfulness, a horse would jump around or threaten to buck or run off. Regardless of his antics, Kyra never got frustrated. She sat as quietly as she would if she was at home in her living room watching television. I could hear her saying over and over again, "That's your problem, not mine." She neither got upset nor took a horse's behavior personally. As a result, she was able to sort through difficulties much more quickly than she would have if she had become frustrated or angry.

I brought Kyra's lesson home with me. Whenever one of my horses offers any number of resistances or evasions, I say to myself, "That's your problem, not mine." This mindset allows me to go about my business without getting emotionally involved. As a result, I am able to get my job done much more effectively.

Another tool I use to stay emotionally detached when I ride my own horses is to pretend that they belong to someone else. This method helps me because, for some mysterious reason, I seem to know exactly what to do when I train other people's horses. I have a clear plan, and if I need to modify that plan, I can do it easily.

CASE HISTORY

JJ

Judy Hanna, known to her friends as JJ, is one of the most confident, competent horsewomen I know. Whenever I have difficulty clearly seeing horse training issues or health problems, I always bounce my thoughts off JJ. I know I can always count on her rational, objective input.

After riding other people's horses for many years, JJ finally purchased her own horse, Maverick. Interestingly enough, she fell victim to the same emotional

Kyra Kyrklund on Flyinge Amiral

JJ Hanna riding Maverick

involvement that I struggle with. She obsessed and second-guessed herself about many of her decisions. She agonized about whether to ride Maverick very energetically forward or sub-power. Should she ride him "deep" with his neck low, or "up" with his poll the highest point? Should she enter some shows to give him exposure, or stay home and train him longer until they become a real team?

JJ was puzzled by her own attitude because she knew if someone else had asked for her opinion, she'd be able to see the big picture clearly and feel confident about making a plan. The issue here had nothing to do with her ability. Her dilemma had its roots in her deep emotional involvement with Maverick. She was afraid to make a mistake. She was worried that if she kept changing her program, she'd confuse him, be unfair to him, or even ruin him.

My advice to her was to "sell" Maverick to her parents for one dollar. I knew that once Maverick "belonged" to someone else, JJ would be able to school him with the same confidence that she has when she rides other people's horses.

Frustration to Serenity

TIPS FOR CHANGE

- Do breathing-relaxation exercises such as the *sleeping dog* (p. 86).
- Recognize and *celebrate little victories.*
- Give yourself an *attitude adjustment.*
- Stay detached by adopting an attitude of "That's your problem, not mine."
- Stay *emotionally detached* by pretending to "sell" your horse to someone for one dollar!

5

The Subconscious Mind

So far, I've given you some simple and easy tips for change: how to set worthwhile goals; stay motivated; use *Getting the NAC* to alter your behavior, emotions, feelings, and riding habits. At this point, I'm going to discuss what I consider one of the most powerful tools for growth and development—as a rider and as a person. It is learning how to *program your subconscious mind*.

In *That Winning Feeling!* I introduced the importance of the subconscious mind in determining how you act and what you do. In this book, I'm going to explore this concept in much further depth. As I said in the introduction to this book, I had always been the type of person who thought that as long as I was determined and persistent, I could accomplish anything that I set my mind to doing. Whether it was starting a new project, dieting, or quitting smoking, I could rely solely on my willpower to reach my goal.

When I tried using willpower to achieve my riding goals, however, I found that progress was either frustratingly slow or nonexistent. No matter how much iron-jawed determination I used, I still had a problem controlling my position on my horse, and even though I worked hard to be calm and cool, I was still tense the days before and during competitions.

It occurred to me that there had to be a better way, not only to reach my goals but, more importantly, to enjoy the process. My research led me to several books that offered the same startling message: Contrary to my beliefs, in the long run, my *conscious* mind ultimately has less influence on my actions, attitudes, and performance; it's my *subconscious* mind that really determines behavior.

Your outer, conscious mind is only the tip of the iceberg.

To understand the difference between the conscious and the subconscious mind, it might be helpful for you to think of your mind as an iceberg. While you're aware of your outer (conscious) mind, it's only the tip of the iceberg. The part with the greater impact is your inner (subconscious) mind, the hidden part of the iceberg.[1] Even though you aren't aware of your subconscious, it really is the part of your mind that controls your actions. It is designed to take "orders" from your conscious mind—it listens to your words and tries to make whatever you say or think come true.[2] Basically, the conscious mind determines *what* you're going to do, and the subconscious mind figures out *how* it's going to happen. In other words, the conscious mind is the *source of thought*, while the subconscious is the *source of power*.[3]

Ultimately, you will achieve whatever your subconscious mind believes. The actions you have taken in your life and the subsequent results were created by the thoughts you deposited—on a daily basis—into your subconscious mind. Your subconscious is responsible for both your successes and your failures.

I also learned that if I relied on conscious willpower to reach a goal, I might be able to make a short-term change, but it would only become a temporary change. If I directed my energy to my subconscious mind, I could make a permanent change. Take dieting, for example. Whenever I decided to lose weight, I was successful as long as I used (extreme!) willpower and rigidly stuck to a diet. However, my success was usually short-lived, and eventually, like so many people, I would gain the weight back.

As long as you *subconsciously* think of yourself as overweight, you will always regain the weight you *consciously* lost.

Then I learned that in any "battle" between the conscious and the subconscious mind, the subconscious mind always wins. I realized that as long as I subconsciously thought of myself as being overweight, I would always regain the weight I had so "consciously" taken off. In order to keep the weight off permanently, I needed to change the "programming" in my mind so that I saw and thought of myself differently when it came to food. I began to think of food as a way to nourish my body so it could function at peak efficiency rather than a source of comfort when I was emotionally stressed. I trained myself to enjoy feeling "empty" before I went to bed instead of thinking I needed a full stomach to sleep well. I learned that refined sugar can wreak havoc on your body, so I began to call anything with sugar in it, "poison," rather than thinking of sweets as "goodies." I even substituted the word "fat" for the word "cream." As a result, the thought of putting "fat" in my coffee, or of having a nice big bowl of mint chocolate chip ice "fat" really turned me off!

The Guided Missile

Your subconscious mind directs you as if you're a *guided missile* to any target. When you "consciously" give your subconscious mind instructions, it will relentlessly, inexorably send you to that target. If you start to veer off course, it automatically makes the necessary corrections to get you back on track.[4] The subconscious mind also doesn't make value judgments. It accepts whatever you tell it, whether or not what you say is true or false. You'll always get a result consistent with whatever this "inner" mind is programmed to make happen.

Not only does your subconscious mind disregard the truth or falsity of what it's told, it also doesn't care if the goal you give it is in your best interests, or not.[5] It just needs a target. So, when you say things like, "I freeze up when people watch me ride," or "I get so nervous, I end up being a passenger," your subconscious mind says, "Oh, goody! A goal! I'll make sure you freeze up when you ride in front of people and that you're so nervous, you end up being a passenger on your horse."

To sum up, your subconscious mind has nothing better to do than wait for your instructions— true or false, positive or negative. So be careful what you wish for, because you just might get it!

Be careful what you wish for; you just might get it!

Dominant Thought

You can also use the power of *dominant thought* to create change. It is a simple and easy tool. Your *dominant thought* can be whatever you think about most of the time, believe in most strongly, truly expect to happen, or imagine most vividly. Your subconscious mind works like a magnet and will always attract your *dominant thought.* By doing this, you can create reality with whatever you choose to focus on. Any thought, good or bad, that you consistently hold in your mind, will materialize as "action" eventually. In fact, what often seems like a coincidence is not really a coincidence at all, but simply your *dominant thought* materializing.

Negative *dominant thoughts* can work against you. If you focus on your horse shying at a rock, he's more likely to do it. If you focus on him knocking down a rail while jumping, that's what will probably happen. If you expect to forget your reining pattern, jump course, or dressage test, chances are you will.

Yet, training yourself to have the right dominant thought will help you manufacture what you want. That is, if you focus on having an attentive, willing partner, he probably will be. If you focus on having a brilliant round, you're more apt to make it happen. If you focus on remaining calm and cool under all kinds of pressure, you surely will be.

The bottom line is that you will automatically move toward your *dominant thought.* Even if you're thinking about something you don't want, you'll gravitate toward it. This is because your mind always moves you toward your thoughts—never away from them.[6]

Eliminate the Word "Don't"

Denis Waitley, author of *The Psychology of Winning*, elaborates on this concept of the mind moving toward things by saying that the mind can't focus on the "reverse" of an idea. You can't move *away* from being fat. You can only move *toward* being thin. You can't move *away* from poverty. You can only move *toward* wealth.

So focus on what you want in your life rather than what you don't want. If you ask a racecar driver how he is able to get through a tight gap without hitting anything, he'll tell you, "Look where you want to go, not where you don't want to go. If you look at the wall, chances are, you'll hit it."[7] When you give yourself instructions that start with the word "don't" such as "Don't pull on the reins," "Don't stiffen," or "Don't be afraid," you are doomed to fail. You can't *move away* from pulling on the reins. You can only *move toward* keeping your hands still. You can't *move away* from being stiff. You can only *move toward* being supple. You can't *move away* from fear. You can only *move toward* courage.

It might help you grasp how using the word "don't" can backfire if you understand that the mind works in pictures. (See *Visualization Can Even Improve a "Bad" Memory*, p. 66.) That's why it's so important to phrase your goals in a positive way. As I explained in Chapter 3, there is no picture in the mind for the word "not." So when your *dominant thought* is, "I do not want to knock down Fence 3," your mind gives you a picture of knocking it down.

Your mind works in pictures, and there's no picture for the word "not," so the outcome above was predictable!

Change Your Software

In order to create change, you need to *change the software* in your subconscious mind. Think of your mind as if it's a computer, and it can only be as useful as its software. By repeatedly reprogramming your mental computer with the right thoughts, words, and pictures, you replace old, negative, self-defeating programming with the kind of new software that helps you reach your goal.

Not only does this repeated programming help you reach your goal, but your success is *guaranteed!* This is because the subconscious mind always reacts to its strongest programming. When this newly loaded information becomes firmly etched in your mind, it ends up being a permanent part of your software, and you have no option but to act in a way consistent with it.

Later in this book, I will show you different ways of using *visualization* and *self-talk* to reprogram your computer by *changing your software* (p. 184).

To create change, reload the software to reprogram your mental computer.

Self-Image

An important element of *changing your software* is *changing your self-image*. You won't be able to change the way you behave—in riding or living—until you change the way you see yourself.

In *That Winning Feeling!* I introduced Maxwell Maltz, author of the groundbreaking book, *Psychocybernetics.* Maltz recognized the importance of the self-image. He said, "Our self-image, strongly held, essentially determines what we become...therefore, the goal of any psychotherapy is to change an individual's image of himself."

Your self-image is the blueprint that determines exactly how you act. Everything you think and do stems from how you see yourself. Because you believe this image to be the truth, you live completely within its boundaries. So, if you're not satisfied with how you're riding (or the quality of your life, for that matter), the first thing you must do is *change your self-image.*

The Comfort Zone

Changing your self-image can be a daunting task. This is because we tend to stubbornly view ourselves a certain way, and we like to stay in our *comfort zone.* The *comfort zone* is safe and secure. Stepping outside of it makes us anxious or uncomfortable, so we come up with all sorts of reasons to avoid doing so. These reasons are usually very logical and hard to dispute. We tell ourselves, "Gee, I'd love to qualify for the finals, but my horse isn't fancy enough to be competitive," or "I know I could be a much better rider, but I can't afford to take lessons on a regular basis," or "I can't make much progress because I'm too busy to ride consistently."

The Achievement Zone

In spite of the fact that leaving our *comfort zone* makes us anxious, we're still occasionally tempted to step outside of it into the *achievement zone.* We venture there partly because never feeling challenged gets boring. An even bigger lure is the sense of accomplishment you feel when you "stretch" yourself. Think about the first time you cantered and jumped, the first time you rode in a show, or the first time you mastered a challenging maneuver. What a rush, wouldn't you say? In hindsight, you'd probably agree that the feeling of accomplishment was well worth the discomfort you felt when you stepped out of your *comfort zone*.

If that feeling is so great, why don't you always "go for it?" It often boils down to your having an insecure self-image. After all, if you really believed you couldn't fail, what would stop you from going after your dreams and goals?

Your Self-Image Thermostat

We have many different thermostats and each has a range that we're comfortable in. For instance, my external body temperature thermostat is happy between sixty-four and seventy-two degrees. Many people find that temperature to be a little on the cool side, but when I walk into my house and the temperature is eighty degrees, I immediately turn on the air conditioner. On the other hand, if I walk into my house and it's fifty-eight degrees, I turn the heat on. I regulate the room temperature so that I can stay happily within my *comfort zone*—neither too hot nor too cold.

Your *self-image thermostat* works in much the same way. Its limited parameters entice you to stay within the very narrow range of your *comfort zone* where you feel secure, and, as a result, you're discouraged from changing. If you are confident, calm, and self-assured, you'll remain that way. If you're insecure, worried, and lacking confidence, you'll stay that way too. Ultimately, your self-image has a huge influence on how well you ride and train, so in order to have a larger *comfort zone* you need to broaden your *self-image thermostat's* range of degrees. To that end, in Chapters 7 and 11, I review the concepts of *visualization* and *self-talk* that I touched on in *That Winning Feeling!* Later on, I explore both of these tools in more depth.

Essentials of the Subconscious Mind

- If you want to make permanent changes, direct your efforts to your subconscious mind rather than your conscious mind. Your subconscious truly controls your actions.
- Your subconscious mind controls you like a *guided missile*. It's just waiting for your instructions. Be sure to choose the right target!
- Your subconscious mind works like a magnet and always attracts your *dominant thought.*
- Create your own reality by controlling your *dominant thought.*
- The mind cannot focus on the reverse of an idea. You can never move *away* from something you don't want. You can only move *toward* something you want.
- Eliminate the word "don't" from your instructions to yourself.
- *Change the software* in your mental computer by repeatedly reprogramming your mental computer with the right thoughts, words, and pictures. You'll do this through *visualization* and *self-talk* (see p. 184).
- Your self-image is the blueprint that determines exactly how you act, so change has to start with adjusting how you see yourself.
- Spice up your life by daring to step out of your *comfort zone* and into the *achievement zone*.

6

Lacking Empathy

The ability to be sympathetic is essential if you want to be a good horseman. That's not to say that an unsympathetic rider can't train a horse, but the dynamics will be such that the best you can hope for is a dictatorial relationship and a mechanical performance.

The sympathetic rider shows empathy for her horse. This is necessary if you're going to turn an animal who, by nature, survives by flight, into a partner who trusts you and lets you lead him. Empathy will also allow you to devise a training program suited to a horse's individual needs and personality rather than forcing him into a rigid system.

So just what is empathy? Empathy means that you try to understand the nature of the horse and are able to think, feel, and act in ways that respect both his distinctiveness as a species, and as an individual. It means you can put yourself into his mind and understand how and why he acts the way he does.

First and foremost, you need to always keep in mind that the primary characteristic of the horse as a species is that of a "prey animal." Much of the behavior that we don't like is simply his survival instinct operating in high gear. His genetic makeup programs him to survive by fleeing from real (or imagined) danger, so by nature, a horse is afraid and insecure. Otherwise, the species would have disappeared a long time ago.

The power to flee and being part of a herd gives a horse a sense of security. In the herd, he follows a leader who tells him when and where to run. By relying

on this leader, he doesn't have to live in a constant state of anxiety, constantly burning up energy running away from potential threats.

It stands to reason, therefore, that a successful partnership between you and your horse results from your ability to take on this role of leader and find ways to make your horse feel secure. As the leader, you make him feel safe enough so he can concentrate on the tasks you put before him. It's only when you provide this feeling of security that he can truly blossom.[1]

How can you tell if you're lacking empathy? Think about the primary emotions you experience when you ride and train:

Do you feel as if the horse is some lesser creature that you need to dominate?

Do you expect your horse to be like a machine that reacts in the same way every day?

Are you irritated, annoyed, frustrated, or even angry much of the time? Are you quick to react by hitting your horse with the whip, jabbing him with spurs, or jerking him in the mouth?

Do you get impatient when he shies or bolts?

Do you try to force every horse into the same, rigid system?

Does it bother you when your horse doesn't want to leave his buddies, or whinnies to them when you're trying to compete?

Do you punish your horse for just being a horse?

Here are two tools you can use to become more empathetic: *ask a better question* and *model top riders*.

Ask a Better Question

First, if you tend to get annoyed or angry at your horse for his insecurities, think about the kinds of questions you're asking. Maybe you ask unsympathetic questions like, "Why are you such a chicken?" "What is the matter with you?" or "Why don't you just knock it off?"

To become a better partner, you need to *ask a better question*. Your better questions will change your focus and, as a result, you're going to have a better attitude toward your horse.[2] How about asking, "How do I design a program to allow you to blossom?" "Would more hay and less grain, or more turnout, reduce your anxiety?" "What's the best training approach for you?" or "How can I help you to be happy and proud of yourself?"

Anky van Grunsven on Gestion Bonfire

All of these questions revolve around respecting the horse as an individual with his own character and needs. Anky van Grunsven, Olympic Gold medal winner in Sydney in 2000, agrees that you must recognize your horse as an individual with his own personality and idiosyncrasies. That quality is what makes her one of the most empathetic (and successful) dressage trainers in the world.

As Anky puts it, "Every horse has his own personal way. I don't ride them all the same because they are not all the same. Every horse is different. They are just like people. One wants to work a little more and another doesn't. One is more brave. Another is more timid. They all have their way of thinking and being, and you must respect how they are. The main thing is that you must be concerned with how your horse thinks and not treat him as if he is a bicycle or a car."

Janice

One of my students, Janice, had always been an "angry" rider. She had a short fuse and was quick to punish her horse, Jasper, when she felt he was uncooperative, or just wasn't trying hard enough. While punishing him sharply, she'd yell out questions like, "How come you're always trying to cheat?" or "Why are you so lazy?" You can see where her focus was when she was asking questions like these.

It might seem like a contradiction considering how she acted when she rode, but Janice really loved Jasper. When she was finished riding, she always regretted how unreasonable and abusive she had been. So, I talked to her about changing her focus and her attitude by coming up with a more empathetic question—this time to herself. What would Jasper say about her if he was able to talk? Janice was sad to admit that he'd probably say that he wasn't very happy. He might say things like, "I'm a little sore on my right hind leg today, and it hurts me to use it," or, "Ugh! Another day of being tortured," or, "I'm confused. I'm trying as hard as I can, but I just don't understand what she wants me to do."

The insight Janice got from walking a mile in Jasper's shoes was enough for her to change her approach to training. Her new guiding question became, "If my horse could talk, what would he say about the way I ride and train him?" She wanted the answer to be that he loved and trusted her, that he loved the time they spent together, and that he would turn himself inside out trying to please her.

You can gain insight by walking a mile in your horse's shoes.

Modeling Top Riders

Another way to become more empathetic is to *model* a top trainer. *Modeling* is fairly simple. All you need to do is find a rider you admire, figure out how he or she acts, and do the same.[3]

Two trainers that I personally *model* are Cindy Sydnor and Klaus Balkenhol. Cindy is a dressage teacher, trainer, competitor, and judge from Snow Camp, North Carolina. She has been one of the major influences in my riding and in the evolution of my teaching methods. She is incredibly creative in both her teaching and her training, and has a wealth of interesting and challenging exercises to help develop the horse as an athlete. She knows that developing physical strength is something that happens gradually, so patience is the hallmark of her method. Also, she never forces a horse into a rigid system, but is fascinated with discovering which approach or exercise will help a

Cindy Sydnor

particular horse understand what she's asking in the kindest, clearest way possible. She lives by the philosophy, "Ask often, expect little, reward generously." She always feels it's a good day when she can teach her horse just one small thing and help him feel content and relaxed in his job.

Klaus Balkenhol has been an Olympic and World Champion riding for Germany on many occasions. At the time of this writing, he is the coach of the United States dressage team and is one of the kindest human beings I've ever had the privilege of knowing. He brings this compassion and sensitivity to his dealings with both people and horses, and this contributes to the tremendous success that our dressage team has enjoyed recently. In fact, under Klaus' tutelage,

Klaus Balkenhol on Goldstern

our team "broke through the bronze ceiling" and, for the first time, won a silver medal in international competition at the World Equestrian Games in Jerez, Spain in 2002.

I *model* so much of what Cindy and Klaus do. They are both elegant, quiet riders. They are fair and systematic in their approach to training. And, above all, they show unbelievable empathy and love for their horses. They understand how

Woody

naturally insecure the horse is and they do everything they can to become a compassionate leader that the horse can rely on for direction.

Cindy understands how the horse's need for security drives him to behave in certain ways. She explains, "People forget about the predator issue because people are now the biggest predators on earth. We forget what it's like to worry that there might be something behind a bush that's going to eat you." She adds, "I particularly admire Klaus Balkenhol's ability to make his horses feel secure so that their natural beauty can emerge. I think that Klaus is one of the best riders in the world, in part because he makes his horses feel so safe. He has the ability to say, 'I'm going to watch out for you. You're fine. You're safe with me.'"

So, to develop a better relationship with your horse, change your attitude by following Klaus's lead. Rather than getting frustrated when your horse shies, for example, adopt an attitude that says, "Trust me. I'll take care of you. You can rely on me to protect you."

I learned the value of making my horse feel safe as I was developing my partnership with Eastwood. When I got "Woody" at age six, he was a very insecure horse. Hacking him was a real challenge. Whenever he saw anything remotely scary, he would wheel to the left and run away. His motto was "Every man for himself!" I never punished Woody for wheeling and running. I'd just quietly turn him around and head back in our original direction. When we finally made it by whatever had frightened him, I always made a big fuss over him.

Nine months after Woody came into my life, this approach paid off. One day, I was preparing to shoot some footage for *The Half-Halt Demystified!* videos. The camera crew had set up their equipment between the two dressage arenas at my home base, Huntington Farm in Strafford, Vermont. All kinds of equipment, like scaffolding and tents with flapping sides, suddenly appeared. Even the most seasoned horses reacted to this sudden change in their peaceful environment.

I rode Woody out to the arena, and as soon as he saw all the paraphernalia and people, he stopped dead in his tracks. I was excited by that reaction in itself. This was the first time that Woody had actually held his ground rather than spinning around and taking off before the "monsters" could get him. I let him stand quietly for a few moments to take the sight in, and gave him a piece of sugar. Then, I closed my legs and asked him to go forward in the direction of the camera crew. I felt him take a deep breath, and he bravely marched forward. In just a few minutes, we were trotting figure-eights around the equipment!

I was so proud of him. That was the moment I knew he had truly become my horse. He trusted me enough to overcome his fear and let me guide him. That moment was actually more exciting for me than anything I taught him over the six years he was in my life including his first series of flying changes every stride, his first piaffe, or even his first passage!

Lacking Empathy to Being Sympathetic

TIPS FOR CHANGE

The sympathetic rider not only understands the nature of the horse as a species but also respects him as an individual.

To become more sympathetic:

- Walk a mile in your horse's shoes.
- Learn how to *ask a better question.*
- *Model top riders.* Find empathetic riders. Figure out how they think and act and then do the same.

7

The Power of Visualization

Previews of Coming Attractions

Visualizing images, not only of how you physically want to look when you ride, but also of how supple and centered you want to *feel* when you ride, will eventually help your riding evolve to match the picture in your mind. I call these pictures *previews of coming attractions* because you're creating your own reality by repeating desired images in your mind's eye.

Elite athletes, around the world and in many different sports, have been using visualization to enhance their performances for a long time. Successful skiers "see" their runs down the mountain before they ever leave the starting gate. Top golfers "see" their shots before they make their swing. In fact, the most common denominator of all elite athletes and superachievers is that they have developed the ability to clearly see what they want, in great detail, well before they actually achieve it. Larry Mahan, champion rodeo rider says, "I try to picture a ride in my mind before I get on a bull, and then I go by the picture."

I remember watching Dwight Stones, Olympic high jumper, go through his pre-jump ritual. Stones would nod his head in time with each step as he "watched" himself run toward the bar. As he saw himself start his run, he would bob his head slowly. As he progressively picked up speed, his head would move faster and faster. Finally, he'd raise his chin high, and then slowly drop it, as he saw himself lifting up and over the bar. All of this would be done while he was standing still. He successfully completed every jump—in his mind's eye—before he did it for real.

The benefits of visualization are not reserved for Olympic athletes, however. Visualization is the finest tool that you have for creating changes. The reason it works is because, as with *modeling* a rider you admire, the subconscious mind does not distinguish between real practice and imagined practice. This mental picture, imagined in great detail, acts like a magnet attracting the attention of the subconscious, which in turn sets up the ideal circumstances to help you reach your goal. When you repeat your mental pictures over and over, they become part of the brain's mental software and the images become a self-fulfilling prophecy.

Consider the East German bobsled team. They attributed their success at the 1980 Winter Olympics to their use of visualization. Team members reported that they spent significantly more time *mentally* rehearsing than actually training on the run: For every occasion they practiced for real, they successfully negotiated the run one hundred more times in their minds' eyes. [1]

What does the success of the East German bobsled team mean to you? It means that ten minutes spent sitting in an armchair vividly visualizing jumping a triple combination "perfectly" is more productive than thirty minutes in the saddle struggling to find your distances. Visualizing jumping a triple combination "perfectly" will help you more than jumping it poorly while actually on your horse.

Visualization Works on Two Levels

I believe that *visualization* is even more effective for riders than for athletes in other sports because of its dual influence.

First, it helps you, the rider. When you hold a clear picture of how you'd like to ride, the images move from your brain to your body so that you actually sit better and give the aids more effectively. In his book *The Mental Edge*, Kenneth Baum explains, "Researchers have discovered that, in a real sense, visualization puts your body through the paces before you ever walk onto the athletic field. Vivid images produce subtle but real firings along the neural pathways that participate in the physical activities that you are visualizing...In a study published in the journal, *Behavior Therapy*, researchers tracked muscle activity in the legs of skiers who were visualizing a downhill run through the use of an electromyelogram (EMG); the electrical activity in their muscles mirrored what occurs during actual skiing."

Second, visualization affects our animals because they think in pictures just like we do. If you doubt this, think of your dog having a dream. His legs twitch and he barks softly as he chases imaginary rabbits in his sleep. Not only do animals think in pictures, but I also believe that they pick up on the pictures that we are holding in our mind's eye. So, I take advantage of this by always visualizing what I want—not what I *don't* want.

Mind's Eye Movie

Here's how I use visualization to tell my horse how I'd like him to do a movement. Let's say I want to improve his leg-yields. In a *mind's eye movie*, I use a *zoom lens* and zero in on his legs (see p. 163). I visualize his legs crossing high up by his knees and hocks. I hold this picture while I'm riding so that not only do my muscles react to the picture, but my horse has a clear image of what I'm asking him to do.

You might argue that his leg yields improve just because I'm giving better aids. I'm sure that's part of it, but I really think it goes beyond that, and the horse is seeing the picture, too. One particularly dramatic example of this was when I practiced piaffe with Zapatero, my mount for the Olympic Trials in 1992. Piaffe should look like a trot on the spot. The horse's legs move energetically up and down in diagonal pairs. Zapatero's piaffe was a bit weak because he didn't always bend his hind legs actively enough. Instead, he sometimes "rope-walked," placing one hind foot directly in front of the other as if he was walking on a tightrope.

When I concentrated and held a clear picture in my mind of Zapatero's hind legs staying apart as he trotted in

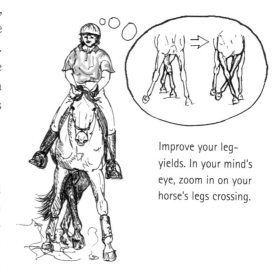

Improve your leg-yields. In your mind's eye, zoom in on your horse's legs crossing.

Zapatero

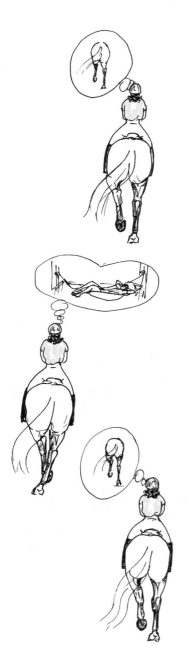

place, he did a very correct piaffe. When my mind wandered, he'd rope walk. As soon as I brought my attention back to his hind legs, he'd widen his stance and bend his hind legs actively again. During the entire movement, I never changed my aids. The only thing that changed was the picture that I held in my mind.

The idea that we communicate with our animals through mental pictures can work against you as well as for you. Say you're out for a hack, and you're riding down the road. As you approach your neighbor's house, you see that she's put her trash out by the road. You think to yourself, "I hope my horse doesn't wheel around and go the other way when he sees those garbage bags." As you're thinking this, you're very vividly visualizing your horse doing just that. Before you know it, your horse is spinning around and heading off in the other direction, and he doesn't understand what you're upset about. After all, you communicated to him that he should spin and bolt. If you want your horse to stay relaxed and march calmly by, you need to transmit a clear picture of him doing just that!

Make sure the aids you give correspond to the picture in your mind. If you give your horse the cue to pick up right-lead canter, picture him picking up that lead, and not the left one. If your body and your mind are giving conflicting signals, like you're asking for right-lead canter, but you're thinking, "Oh, no. Don't make a mistake," you're giving contradictory cues, and the chances are your horse will be confused and end up making the error.

But I Can't Visualize

If you're concerned that you're not a good "visualizer," that this technique is going to be hard for you to use, think about how often you daydream. Well, when you daydream, you're visualizing.

When I focused on Zapatero's hind legs, he did a very correct piaffe...when my mind wandered, his hind legs would cross...and when I brought my attention back to his hind legs, he would become correct again.

If you worry that your horse will wheel around when he sees something scary, like garbage bags...

...chances are he will do exactly that.

But, if you picture him marching calmly by...

...this is what he'll do instead.

Or, think about how often you worry. Do you worry that your horse will be so fresh at the first show of the season that you'll get bucked off? Do you agonize over whether you're ruining your horse because you're not a good enough rider? Are you anxious that you'll "freeze" if you ride in front of a large group of people? Do you worry that you won't be able to come up with the money for the entry fee for a show?

If you've ever worried about anything at all, you're in luck. That's because worrying is just *negative* use of imagination. When you worry, you picture *in great detail* all the horrible things that might happen. So, if you tend to be the type of person who worries, take heart. You'll be particularly good at using visualization to improve your riding.

If you're still concerned that you won't be able to visualize effectively, try the following exercises to prove to yourself how easy and natural it is to make mental pictures.

First, describe your living room sofa. Maybe you'll say it's brown and beige tweed with big overstuffed cushions and some dog hair on it. Did you actually spell out the words b-r-o-w-n-a-n-d-b-e-i-g-e-t-w-e-e-d? Or did you conjure up a picture of your sofa, and then look at that picture in order to describe it?

Now, imagine that you're standing in your tack room. In your mind's eye, see yourself doing a slow, 360-degree turn. Describe what you see. How many saddle and bridle racks are there? How many windows? Are the windows clean? Do they have curtains? What color are the curtains? Are there hooks for clothes? Is there a clock? What sizes and colors are the tack trunks? Are there any pictures or ribbons on the walls? Is there a bulletin board? Is there any furniture in the room? What does the furniture look like?[2]

In order to describe your tack room in such detail, you had to use visualization. These simple exercises prove that you already think in pictures. Now, all you need to do is use what comes naturally and apply it to your riding goals.

Visualization Can Even Improve a "Bad" Memory

Have you ever claimed that you have a lousy memory? You might lament that you tend to forget people's names the moment after you've met them. You forget your reining pattern, your dressage test, or you blank out and actually go off course when you're jumping. In truth, there is nothing wrong with your memory. Take the following test to see how the power of visualization seems to instantly improve a "bad" memory.

Quickly read through the following list:

1. Tree
2. Light Switch
3. Stool
4. Car
5. Glove
6. Gun
7. Dice
8. Skate
9. Cat
10. Bowling ball
11. Goal post
12. Eggs

Now close the book, take a piece of paper and number the left side of the paper: One to Twelve. Write down as many of the items on the list as you can and in the order in which you read them.

How many did you remember, and did you have them in the right order?

Let's go through the list again, but this time, you're going to visualize each of the items in order.

Number One is *tree*. Picture a tree. The trunk of the tree looks like the number one. What kind of tree is it? A weeping willow? A mighty oak? Is it autumn and the leaves have turned brilliant colors, or is it winter and the branches are bare?

Number Two is *light switch*. A light switch has two positions. Up/down. On/Off. What kind of light switch is it? Does it have a decorative frame around it? Is it in the bathroom? Is it in the kitchen?

Number Three is *stool*. A stool has three legs. Is it a small footstool? Or is it a long legged bar stool? Is the seat padded, or is the stool made entirely of wood?

Number Four is *car*. A car has four doors; four tires. Is the shift a "four on the floor?" Maybe you'll see a "FOURd"! What color and model is this Ford?

Number Five is *glove*. A glove has five fingers. Is it a white glove for showing? Or, is it a crocheted-back glove for schooling? Is the glove so well-used that some of the tips of the fingers have worn through?

Number Six is *gun*. If you get shot by one of these, you'll be "six feet under." Think of a six-shooter with its six chambers in the cylinder. What does the hand grip look like? Is it pearl-handled? Is there checkering on it? Is the name of the manufacturer on it? Does it have a custom grip to fit your hand?

Number Seven is *dice*. Lucky seven! Think of rolling the dice and exclaiming, "Seven come eleven!" Are you rolling the dice in a casino in Las Vegas? Is it the Sands? Can you see all the neon lights? The slot machines?

Number Eight is *skate.* Eight rhymes with skate. What kind of skates do you see? Ice skates? Roller skates? Can you see yourself doing figure-eights with your skates?

Number Nine is *cat.* A cat has nine lives. What kind of cat do you see? A Siamese? A tiger? Is the cat sleeping by the cat-o'-nine-tails?

Number Ten is *bowling ball*. When you knock down ten pins, you get a strike. There are ten frames in a game. You can use the little balls called "candle pins" or the big balls called "ten pins." What does the ten-pin bowling alley look like? Are there leagues playing with teams wearing matching shirts?

Number Eleven is *goal post*. The sides of the goal post look like the number eleven. There are eleven players on the field in a football game. Is it the Super Bowl? What color is your team's uniform? Where are you sitting in the stands?

Number Twelve is *eggs*. There are twelve eggs in a carton. Are they brown or white? Are they cage-free, organic eggs? When you open the carton, are any of the eggs broken or cracked?

Now, get out your piece of paper again and number it from one to twelve. Write down as many of the words as you can in the right order. Are you astounded by how many you got right this time? It's not that your memory instantly improved; you were able to remember more of the list because you used the power of *visualization* to help you.[3]

Fool Your Subconscious Mind

Since, as you now know, the subconscious mind can't tell the difference between what is real and what is vividly imagined, you can therefore lie to your subconscious and become a better rider. Lying can help you achieve your goals much more easily than using the iron-jawed determination that comes with conscious effort.

To fool your subconscious and make changes in two areas—improving your skills and creating the right attitude or mind set—I'll discuss how to enhance a skill in *Perfect Practice* next, and how to improve your attitude in *Change Your Attitude*, which follows.

Perfect Practice

Consider a study that was done in the Soviet Union that supports the importance of the mental side of sports. In this study, the Soviets, who were preparing for the 1980 Winter Olympic Games, were assigned to one of four training programs. The first group was made up of athletes who spent one hundred percent of their time on physical training. The second group devoted seventy-five percent of its time to physical training and twenty-five percent to mental training. The third group divided its time equally between physical and mental regimens. The final group spent twenty-five percent on the physical aspects of training and seventy-five percent on the mental side.

The results were amazing. The more time that athletes devoted to mental training, the more they improved. Those who made the greatest strides spent the majority of their time (seventy-five percent) mentally preparing, while the least amount of progress was seen in the athletes who worked exclusively on physical training.[4]

Practice doesn't make perfect, unless it's *perfect* practice.

How does this study relate to developing particular riding skills? Take, for example, a canter depart. Each day you get on your horse and practice transitions from trot to canter. During the transition, your horse stiffens his back, raises his neck, and trots faster and faster until he finally breaks into the canter. Not a pretty picture, is it? Technically, it is what is known as a "crummy" canter depart!

How can you possibly expect your transitions to get better when all you practice are worthless canter departs? You see, it isn't completely true that practice makes perfect. It's *perfect* practice that makes perfect. In order to get better you need to practice riding only high quality transitions.

Here's how you can negate those ten worthless canter transitions you've done while riding your horse: In the comfort of your living room, relax, close your eyes and visualize in great detail one hundred soft, relaxed, fluid, obedient canter transitions. Since your subconscious mind can't tell the difference between the ten crummy transitions you actually did on your horse and the hundred beautiful ones you did in your imagination, you will improve. It's simply a numbers game. As far as your mind is concerned, you've actually done ten times as many good transitions as bad transitions.

Change Your Attitude Through Visualization

In Chapter 15, *Attitude is Everything*, I discuss the importance of attitude. For now, let's look at how you can improve your attitude with visualization. What's your emotional challenge? For instance, do you get nervous at shows? Are you timid on the cross-country course? Do you often get frustrated or impatient when training your horse?

If this sounds like you, you can change your programming fairly quickly with detailed mental pictures. Over and over again, vividly visualize yourself as a calm and poised competitor, an aggressive cross-country rider, or an endlessly calm and patient trainer. In your mind's eye, practice acting the way you'd like to be in reality. It might seem as if you're lying to yourself, but, remember, as far as your subconscious mind is concerned, your images are simply *previews of coming attractions.*

When I compete, I use this type of rehearsal to prepare myself mentally so that I'm in the right mindset by the time the competition rolls around. I start three weeks before a show because I've learned that it takes twenty-one days to develop a habit. This is true for a *good* habit as well as a *bad* habit. Not only do I do *perfect practice* rehearsing my tests stride-for-stride, seeing the "perfect" ride in my mind's eye, but I also practice experiencing the attitude and emotions I want in order to have a great ride. Here's how I do it:

I begin outside the dressage arena. I ask my horse to pick up the canter and as my horse obediently reacts to my light aids, I "see" myself looking calm and poised. More importantly, I get fully associated to the image by remembering another time in my life when I actually felt calm and poised, and I conjure up that feeling again. We're relaxed, in harmony, and ready to enter the ring.

Just before I enter the ring itself, I let a feeling of gratitude wash over me. "I'm so lucky to be healthy enough today to be here doing what I enjoy with this animal that I love." I believe that taking a moment to feel grateful is an important part of having "That Winning Feeling." It seems silly to complain that it's too hot, too cold, too windy, the footing is lousy, you hate the stabling, or the judges hate your horse. Keep competition in perspective. It's just a horse show. You could be confined to a wheelchair or heading off to the hospital for chemotherapy. Yet, here you are, spending the day with your horse. How lucky you are, indeed. (See *attitude of gratitude*, p. 131.)

The moment I enter the ring, however, my *attitude-of-gratitude* persona is replaced by a warrior-athlete mindset. I look the judge in the eye and say to myself, "Lucky you! You've been sitting there all day, bored to tears. Well, you'd just better check your socks, Buster, because by the time I'm done, I'm gonna knock 'em off!"

Wow! Calmness, gratitude, and the "eye of the tiger" all before the first salute. I'm programming myself with the emotions and attitudes that will set me up for a confident, dynamic ride.

You, too, can use the power of visualization to do this. What's holding you back from riding at a higher standard? Do you see yourself as timid, uncoordinated, impatient, insecure, lacking confidence, or too aggressive?

I'll remind you once more: The subconscious mind—the part of your mind that ultimately determines your actions—can't tell the difference between what's real and what you practice in your imagination. So, in your *mind's eye movies*, practice being brave, patient, confident, aggressive, and secure, or anything else you want to be, and these attributes will be yours.

Combine Real Practice with Mental Rehearsal

Visualization is not a substitute for saddle time, of course. You still need to develop your seat as well as learn the aids for specific movements. Visualization is simply a means of enhancing your riding and training and accelerating your progress toward goals.

In Andrew Matthews' book, *Being Happy*, he explains how this works. Matthews explains that, "The fastest way to improve is to combine regular physical with regular mental practice. Recent scientific discoveries prove that when you imagine yourself performing a task, you alter your mental programs just as you do when you actually perform it. Your brain undergoes electro-chemical changes within its cells, which produce new behavior...We want these patterns on our brain cells to be as close to perfect as possible, and the only place you can perform perfectly is in your mind."

Practice Without Pressure

Not only can you do *perfect practice* in your imagination, but an added bonus is that you can *practice without pressure*. You can have some quality, practice time without the normal anxiety that goes along with competing or producing results—for real.[5]

Louise's *perfect practice* homework was to visualize her mount loping calmly through changes like a Western pleasure horse.

CASE HISTORY

Louise

One of my students, Louise, was having trouble teaching her horse to do flying changes. More often than not, the changes themselves were okay, but right after the flying change, Louise's horse would get really tense and bolt forward.

This happened so often that Louise began to anticipate her horse taking off. It reached the point where as soon as she even *thought* about doing changes, she'd get anxious. Of course, when she got anxious, she transferred her tension to her horse. He was then convinced that there was definite cause for alarm. He'd get even more frantic, and the bolting got more dramatic.

I gave Louise some *perfect practice* homework to help her with this issue. Part of her homework was to repeatedly watch videotapes of someone else doing calm, relaxed flying changes. The other part of her homework was to sit in a comfortable chair, take a few deep breaths to help her relax, and then visualize calm flying changes over and over. I wanted her not only to see her horse looking confident and relaxed as he loped through changes like a Western pleasure horse, but also to see herself at ease, both physically and emotionally. I told her to experience her respiration and heart rate remaining normal and her muscles staying loose. I had her feel totally confident that flying changes were something she could do as easily as asking for a transition from walk to trot.

A few weeks after adding *perfect practice* to her real-time practice, Louise and her horse were not only doing relaxed flying changes, they were also starting to do several flying changes in a sequence.

The Power to Heal

Never underestimate the power of visualization to influence your skills, as well as your attitude, while riding. Its power is revealed in startling stories of people who have used visualization to heal themselves, both mentally and physically.

CASE HISTORIES

Martha

Martha told me how she had used visualization in her riding for years with great success, but she was both surprised and thrilled to see how visualization helped her deal with a panic attack. In her letter she wrote, "This past week I was in a place that you might call a "tight spot." I had to go to the hospital for an MRI—a diagnostic examination that involves the patient lying motionless in a narrow, tight, low-ceilinged space. The technician asked if I was claustrophobic. I am a scuba diver and had never had any problems with claustrophobia, so I said no. I was placed in the tube and was fine for the first two or three minutes. Then I started to feel panicked. To stay calm and take my mind off my confinement, I decided to 'ride' a dressage test! At the beginning of every six-minute section, the technician called out, 'Six more minutes.' I rode the first test at supersonic speed. So, I start-

Nancy Bliss Byrd
on Taipan

ed the same test again, but this time I did some *perfect practice* as I concentrated on the details of riding every single movement. Focusing on the fine points of my ride took so long that, forty-five minutes later, as I emerged from the tube, I even needed a few more seconds to finish my salute. It was one of the worst and best moments of my life. Having a panic attack was the worst moment, but 'riding' such a fabulous dressage test was one of the best!"

Nancy

I find the stories of people who have used visualization to heal themselves physically even more astounding. Take, for example, my friend and student, Nancy Bliss Byrd. I introduced Nancy in *That Winning Feeling!* She was a member of the World Championship U.S. Three-Day Event team in 1982. These days, she rides, trains, teaches, competes in dressage, and is the busy mother of two toddlers. Nancy also has multiple sclerosis.

She has done a terrific job taking care of herself over the years. She managed her disease well and had been in remission up until a few years ago when her MS suddenly became active again. Nancy first realized she was having problems because she was having pain in her eye, and her vision was starting to blur. She went to the doctor and he explained that her optic nerve was inflamed and that she needed to be admitted to the hospital. He advised her to postpone a trip she had planned to the Caribbean. He was concerned that the drastic change in temperature from the cold of New England, where she lives, to the warmth of the Caribbean, could make the problem worse.

Never one to crumble in the face of a challenge, Nancy did some research. She went to the library and looked up "optic nerve." Once she had a clear picture of the optic nerve in her mind's eye, she visualized bathing it in cool water. As she bathed it, she saw the nerve go from swollen and red, to less swollen and pink, and finally to a normal size and color.

Nancy repeated this vivid mental picture several times a day. After three days, she called to triumphantly inform me that the pain was gone, her optic nerve had returned to normal, and she didn't need to cancel her trip or go to the hospital.

Joy

I've heard many other incredible stories of the healing power of visualization. One year, I gave a seminar in Spokane, Washington. After describing the power of visualization to the participants, a young woman raised her hand.

Joy had a very moving story to tell. She explained that she had become pregnant with her first baby while she was in her early forties. Everything seemed fine in the beginning, but when she was well into her pregnancy, her doctor told her there was a very serious problem. Apparently, she did not have enough amniotic fluid to keep her baby alive. She was advised to carry the baby to term, but was told that there was no chance that the baby would survive.

Joy proceeded to use visualization to heal herself. Every day she immersed herself in a bathtub filled with warm water. While there, she closed her eyes and imagined warm, soothing, sea-green water gently lapping her stomach. She envisioned that the water bathed and nourished her baby. She added emotion to her imaging. She told the baby that she wanted her to live, but if she didn't, that was okay. She told the baby that no matter what happened, she was deeply loved. She repeated this procedure day after day.

At the time of the seminar, Joy proudly told us that she was the mother of a beautiful, healthy two-year-old daughter.

Now if visualization can heal the mind and the body like that, just think what it can do for your trot lengthenings or combination fences!

Essentials of Visualization

- Use *visualization* to improve both your riding skills and your attitude.

- Think of your mental pictures as *previews of coming attractions.*

- Do *perfect practice* in your mind's eye. Ten minutes spent visualizing "perfect" movements or skills is more productive than thirty minutes in the saddle repeating worthless movements or poorly executed skills.

- The quickest way to improve is to combine regular physical practice with regular mental practice.

- *Perfect practice* allows you to practice without pressure.

- Give yourself time to make changes. It takes twenty-one days to develop a new habit.

8

Impatience

I've known a lot of incredibly talented riders who never seem to fulfill their potential to become great riders. On the other hand, I know even more riders who are less innately gifted but end up becoming very successful. What's the difference? In a nutshell, I'd have to say it's patience and persistence.

I think one of the biggest factors contributing to a lack of patience is having expectations. The same dynamic occurs in many relationships. When we place our own expectations on another being—human or otherwise—we're bound to get impatient from time to time.

We get impatient with our horses when we expect them to:
- act like machines
- think logically
- learn according to human timetables
- never voice an opinion through resistance or evasion
- always be cooperative
- never get distracted or nervous

If you lose your patience while riding, your impatience can escalate into anger, and when you get angry, everyone suffers. Your horse always suffers in the moment, and after the fact, you suffer by feeling guilty that you took your emotions out on your horse. If you really want your horse to be a happy, willing partner, and you want to give him the opportunity to blossom, you need to be endlessly patient.

One of the ways I've learned to become more patient is to learn how to recognize *shades of gray*. I've learned not to expect training to be black and white. Instead, I'm happy when I can make any little bit of progress. My guideline for recognizing these *shades of gray* is the phrase "a little bit better." I'm satisfied anytime my horse can do anything just "a little bit better."

To keep track of the *shades of gray*, I keep a journal of my rides. I ask myself, "Have things been a little bit better, not only within each ride, but also from day-to-day?" When you or your horse seem to be plateauing, you can look back in your book and see where you were last week, last month, or even last year. Your journal will help you keep things in perspective.

For example, maybe I get impatient because my horse doesn't always stay on the bit during every canter depart. But if I look back at my journal, I see that two months ago, I was only getting fifty percent of the transitions on the bit. And, two months before that, not only was he coming off the bit, but he was racing off like a maniac when I asked for the canter. By looking at my journal and seeing our progress, I can stay positive. I don't have the expectation that everything has to be perfect right now. Instead, I'm content with *shades of gray*.

CASE HISTORY

Peggy

Richard Shrake, author of *Resistance Free Riding* and *Resistance Free Training*, epitomizes patience and persistence. All you have to do is spend a few moments in his company and before you know it, you're wrapped in a warm, fuzzy blanket of steadfast calmness. He has that effect on people and animals alike. When I asked him for examples of patience and persistence, Richard told me about a lady, Peggy Van Fleet, who had come to him for lessons. He said:

"We were at a show, and I saw this lady out of the corner of my eye. She was in a trail class, and was totally destroying everything on this big, homely horse. I thought, man oh man, if there's ever a horse who is a square peg in a round hole, it's this one. I walked away, and the next thing I knew she was at my stable telling me not only did she want to go to the World Show where the 'best of the best' compete, but she wanted to be competitive there.

You'll be more patient with your horse if you learn to be satisfied with little bits of progress.

"At the time she was sixty-eight years old. She was from Montana and rode barrels and poles, but she wanted to go to the World Show and win in trails. My immediate reaction was to tell her that I was too busy. The next thing I knew she was at my barn, and she followed me around like a bad cold for at least two weeks. When she finally left, she said, 'I'm going to go home and qualify for the Worlds. Look out!' On July 31, she called and said she had qualified. Then, she scared me to death by asking, 'Richard, would you be my trainer?' I was horrified because I'm picturing this lady destroying all the obstacles, walking out of the ring, putting her arms around me saying 'My Trainer!'

"But, then I thought, by golly, if this sixty-eight year old lady could take that horse and qualify him, she deserves some kind of help. So, we started to work together, and by the end of that year, she made top ten in the amateur division.

"So, at age sixty-nine she went to the World Championship Quarter Horse Show and placed in the top ten a couple of times in amateur trail. Some of those classes had as many as eighty horses in them. For that horse to place was, in itself, a miracle. But, the other thing that added to Peggy's challenge was that she was suffering from terminal cancer. She was going through chemotherapy, and actually was on oxygen right up to the time she went into her classes.

"The following year, Peggy was admitted to the hospital. The doctors said that she only had three weeks to live. But Peggy really wanted to ride her horse at the same show. Her sister called and asked me to come down to try to convince her stay in the hospital. I went there and was so distressed to see this ninety-pound lady who had originally weighed one-hundred-and-eighty pounds. I really didn't think she was going to make it. I tried to talk her out of riding, but she was determined.

"Every trainer around, from Bob Avila, to Steve Metcalf, to Bruce Gilchrist tried to help her out. They bought her an airline ticket, but she didn't want to fly back. She wanted to drive with her horse. She didn't win, but she got a standing ovation at the show. She died three weeks later at the age of seventy.

"Now, here's the key to the whole story. Peggy wasn't healthy, she didn't have a lot of help, she wasn't the right age, she darn sure didn't have the horse, but yet in spite of all those obstacles, she still achieved her goal. Why was she successful? She was patient and persistent with her 'square peg.' She absolutely loved her horse. In her eyes, he could do no wrong. She also had a passion for wanting to achieve her goal. And, she believed in herself. There was no question in Peggy's mind that she wasn't going to get it done."

Whimjammer

Since we live in a culture of immediate gratification and disposable products, patience and persistence can be hard to come by. If something doesn't measure up to our expectations, we get impatient, discard it, and buy the next great product or dream that promises us success. Obviously, Richard doesn't fall into that trap. His patient and persistent methods do not only apply to his students, like Peggy Van Fleet, but also to his horses. He told me about a horse named Whimjammer. "I first bought him as a three-year-old for a client by the name of Anne Marie Munsen. She was a great youth rider, and it was her last year of 'thirteen-and-under.' I wasn't looking for a young horse, but when I saw him move on the longe, I had to buy him. I knew such a green horse was a big gamble, but I took him home and put some time into him. When I thought I had him pretty well together, I started to show him. It was a disaster. I took him to five local shows and didn't get a prize on him. I didn't even get a sixth place ribbon! It was very discouraging, but I believed in him. It never occurred to me to pack it in with him. Besides, my philosophy has always been to give every horse at least ten shots. We haul a horse to ten judges, and only after that much time do we sit back and evaluate him. I don't think it's fair to go to a couple of shows and decide if a horse is okay or not. Even if it's a burro, I give him ten shots!

"The second five times we showed him, we were able to qualify for the World Show. Now, this meant we had to win some six-point classes—classes of over forty horses. Whimjammer either won or was second in every one of them. We qualified him for the World Show, and we took him to the Quarter Horse Congress that fall where he won the All-Around. This horse went on to be a multiple World Champion in not only English but Western. If I'd have given up on him after those first five shows, he would never have become the World Champion he was meant to be. My advice to riders is that you've got to be patient, you've got to be persistent, and you must believe in your horse. Don't let a blue ribbon (or lack of one!) tell you whether your horse is great or not."

Impatience to Patience

- Always remember that patience and persistence are more important than talent.
- To become more patient, learn how recognize *shades of gray*. As long as things get a little bit better, it's time to *celebrate*.
- Start a journal so you can keep track of the *shades of gray*.
- Believe in your horse. Don't let another person's opinion tell you whether or not your horse is great.

9

The Importance of Relaxation

I f you're like most people, there's a lot of stress in your life. You rush around, eat too quickly, drive too fast, struggle to meet deadlines, and generally juggle too many commitments. You long for even a temporary reprieve from all the pressure.

It's probably no surprise to you, then, that relaxation exercises will give you some relief from all the tension in your life. But, you might be interested to know that the same exercises that defuse daily stress can also be very useful for enhancing the visualization skills you learned in the last chapter, as well as helping you to relax when riding.

Relaxation Enhances Visualization

In Chapter 5, you learned about your two minds—the conscious and the subconscious. You discovered that even though you're aware of your conscious mind, it's your subconscious mind that has the greater impact on your actions, attitudes, and performance.

Interestingly enough, even though the subconscious mind plays the bigger role in shaping your behavior, your conscious mind demands most of your attention because it's constantly chattering away at you. A lot of your conscious mind's chatter is harmless. You have innocuous thoughts like, "What am I going to have for dinner?" or "I should stop at the bank on my way home." Often, however, this self-talk is negative or critical which is destructive. You undermine yourself with thoughts like, "I'll never get this," or "I can't believe what an idiot I am," or "I'm so uncoordinated—every time I use my leg, I end up jerking on the reins at the same time."

To get the maximum benefit from visualization exercises, you need to quiet your conscious mind so you can get a more "direct line" to your subconscious. By doing *relaxation exercises*, you can quiet that niggling little voice inside you and become a more effective visualizer. What follows are some of my favorite relaxation techniques that not only *enhance visualization*, but also help you *relax* while you're riding.

Brain-wave pattern One: Beta

Pattern Two: Alpha

The Brain-Wave/Emotion Connection

In order to understand the physiology behind relaxation, you need to know a little bit about brain-wave activity and how it affects your emotions. We all have four basic brain-wave patterns called *beta*, *alpha*, *theta*, and *delta* states. If you are hooked up to an electroencephalogram (EEG), you will see a different pattern for each of these states.

When you're in a *beta* state, there is a high frequency of brain waves. The electrical activity of your brain pulses at between 14 to 40 cycles per second. Picture very dense squiggles almost equal in height being made by the recording arm of the EEG machine. In this state, you might be alert, edgy, uptight, defensive, angry, or afraid.

When you're in an *alpha* state, the frequency of your brain waves is 8 to 13 cycles per second. In an alpha state, you feel relaxed, free, easy, and connected. You'll see that the squiggles on the recording chart are less dense, and after every three or four squiggles, you'll get a sharp spike or peak in brain-wave activity. These bursts of high amplitude come from deeper brain structures, and show that more energy is focused on imagery.

In a *theta* state, brain-wave activity is 4 to 7 cycles per second. In this state, you feel sleepy or like you're floating or drifting.

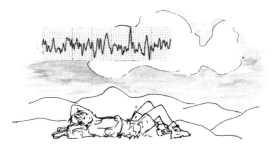

Pattern Three: Theta

Pattern Four: Delta

You can better understand the physiology of relaxation if you learn a little about brain-wave activity and how it correlates with emotions.

A theta state is associated with profound imaging, visions, and dreams.

Finally, in a *delta* state, brain-wave activity is less than 4 cycles per second. This is a sleep state.

For visualization, you want to achieve the deep relaxation associated with a low Alpha/borderline Theta state. For riding, you need to be sharper than that—in a low Beta/borderline Alpha state. In this state, you feel alert yet relaxed, free, at ease, and calm—perfect for riding your horse.[1] (This is also the best state for concentration, which I discuss in *Distraction* on p. 175.)

Relaxation Exercises for Imaging

I'm going to give you several relaxation exercises to choose from in order to achieve the deep relaxation associated with a low Alpha/borderline Theta state. In *Relaxation Exercises for Riding*, I'll give you additional exercises that will help you to get into the low Beta/borderline Alpha state you'll want when you ride.

The first two types of relaxation exercises are called *progressive relaxation* and *autogenic relaxation*. I described them in detail in *That Winning Feeling!* Here's a brief review:

Progressive relaxation involves systematically tensing and relaxing specific muscle groups. With your body relaxed, tense one specific muscle group. Hold that tension, and increase it over the course of several seconds until you feel this group of muscles quivering. Relax completely, and as you do, *anchor* the feeling with *buzzwords* such as "relax" or "let go."

Autogenic relaxation is less physical. You simply think about a group of words and allow these words to have an effect on you. You can either say the words out loud, or you can make a tape of your voice quietly repeating phrases such as, "I am drifting into relaxation," "My body feels heavy and warm," "I feel serene and peaceful." Once you are deeply relaxed, *anchor* this feeling with *buzzwords* such as "easy," "loosen up," or, "I am calm."

It takes about six weeks to learn these techniques, but I feel that the investment in time is well worth it. This is particularly true because once you've learned how to do these exercises, it only takes a few seconds to become deeply relaxed. This is because you *anchor* the feeling of deep relaxation with your *buzzwords*. So, all you have to do to prepare for a *visualization* session, for example, is take a couple of deep breaths, say one or more of your *buzzwords*, and you'll sink into a deeply relaxed state. Your *buzzwords* also come in handy in other situations. I use mine whenever I'm nervous about driving the horse trailer in heavy traffic, or when there's turbulence while I'm on an airplane.

Sonic meditation is another simple way to become relaxed. Simply focus your attention on a particular sound such as that of rain or a stream. There are many audiotapes of nature sounds available, and companies such as Sharper Image have products like the *Heart and Sound* "soother" that has a variety of sounds including rainforest, river, and ocean. As you focus on the sound of the water, let other thoughts drift away. Let the rushing sound of the water deeply relax your body.

Scanning is yet another method. When *scanning,* you use your mind's eye to take an inventory of where you feel tight. Focus your attention on different body parts and become aware of any tension. Concentrate on areas where stress most often hides—forehead, neck, shoulders, jaw, and stomach. As you focus on each of these areas, let a wave of soothing relaxation come over you. Tell your forehead, "Relax." Tell your neck, "Relax." Tell your shoulders, "Relax." Tell your jaw, "Relax." Then, breathe in deeply and let your stomach relax.

You can also relax by simply breathing diaphragmatically. To give yourself an idea of how to do this, watch how a cat or dog breathes when resting. This slow, deep breathing is *belly breathing*. Learning how to *belly breathe* is a fairly simple process if you do this exercise I call the *sleeping dog*. Lie down on the floor and place this book on your abdomen. Take a deep breath through your nose and as you inhale, feel as if you are taking air all the way down into your stomach. Of course, you can't take air into your stomach, but your deep breathing is lowering your diaphragm so you can take more air into your lungs. As a result, your stomach sticks out as if you're getting fat. Breathe in so deeply that when your stomach expands, the book, which is resting on top of your inflated belly, rises. Then, as you exhale through your mouth, your stomach deflates, and the book falls.

One image I like to use when *belly breathing* is to picture that I'm inhaling relaxation and exhaling tension. Another way to picture this is to do *plus/minus signs.* Imagine inhaling *plus* signs through your nose for a slow count of four. Hold your breath for a count of two. Then, exhale *minus* signs through your mouth for a slow count of four. As you inhale the plus signs, visualize taking in positive energy. As you exhale, push negative thoughts out of your body and mind.

Once you've experienced this *belly breathing* while lying on the floor, you're ready to use it anytime you want to relax, and particularly before you practice your imaging. Sit in an easy chair and take two deep breaths. Each time you inhale, feel your abdomen expand. Each time you exhale, feel yourself sinking deeper and deeper into the chair. Inhale relaxation. Exhale tension. Inhale a third time, but this time, hold your breath for a count of ten. As you exhale, feel yourself drifting deeper and deeper into relaxation.

Practice *belly breathing* by watching a cat or dog breathe slowly and deeply when resting: inhale and let your stomach expand, then exhale and let your stomach deflate.

Finally, you can use *deep relaxation* to enhance the relaxed state you've already achieved. In order to deepen your relaxation, say something relaxing as you count slowly backward from ten to one. The words and statements that follow are just to give you an idea of how the method works, but you can come up with your own.

Relaxing Statements

Say the following ten statements:

Ten...I am breathing deeply.

Nine...I feel the relaxation growing.

Eight...I am letting go of tension.

Seven...My arms are getting heavy.

Six...I am more deeply relaxed.

Five...I am drifting into relaxation.

Four...I feel a glowing warmth in my hands and feet.

Three...I am more and more relaxed.

Two...I am drifting deeper into relaxation.

One...I am deeply relaxed.

I usually add some imaging to my counting. Sometimes, I imagine that I'm in an elevator on the tenth floor and I'm slowly descending to the first floor. Other times, I imagine that I'm at the top of an escalator, and as the escalator takes me to the bottom, I slowly count from ten to one.

Relaxation Exercises for Riding

Not only do you need to be able to relax when you're visualizing, but you also need to train yourself to relax when you ride. This is important for two reasons. When you're tense, tight muscles prevent you from sitting well and using your body effectively. Also, your horse will immediately be aware of your mental state, and it's very difficult to do quality work when either you or your horse is tense.

When *belly breathing* while riding, become centaur-like by picturing your seat dissolving into your horse as you exhale.

Since relaxation is so essential to good riding, here are three more relaxation exercises to help you get into the low Beta/borderline Alpha state. The aim of the first exercise, *the centaur,* is to make a conscious effort to breathe deeply at specific times throughout your ride. *The centaur* is a version of *belly breathing*, which I told you about on page 86. The goal of the second exercise, *click the pen*, is to *anchor* a feeling of relaxation with a physical cue. The goal of the third exercise, *squeeze the sponge*, is to *anchor* the ability to slow down your heart rate with a physical cue.

1. For *the centaur,* practice *belly breathing* at specific times during your ride. When breathing deeply, inhale through your nose and feel like you're breathing way down into your stomach. Let your stomach expand as if you're trying to make yourself look fat. Then, *exhale* slowly through your mouth. As you do, feel your butt muscles relax so rather than feeling as if you're perched above or disconnected from your horse, you feel like you're at one with him. Picture your seat dissolving down into your horse's body so you look like a centaur. Consciously breathe like this when you first get on, and continue to do so periodically throughout your ride, as well as during every break to the walk.[2]

   I've made it a habit to do this exercise just before I enter the arena at a show. As I go around the outside of the ring before my dressage test, I take those three deep breaths. With each exhale, I allow my seat to sink deeper and deeper into the saddle. This exercise can be done by riders in all disciplines.

2. In *click the pen,* you *anchor* a feeling of relaxation with the specific physical cue of touching your thumb and forefinger together as if you're clicking the top of a pen to retract or push out the point. This is a particularly practical cue for riders because of the way we hold the reins.

   First, take a deep breath through your nose and hold it. As you hold your breath, make a fist with one hand. Clench that fist as tightly as you can for a few seconds. Next, exhale slowly through your mouth, and as you are exhaling, gradually open your hand and let go of all the tension in your fist. Look at the palm of your hand and visualize the word "relax" written on it. Say "relax" out loud as you "see" the word written on the palm of your hand. Each time you say "relax," let go of any tension in your body. Do this two more times.

   After you say the word "relax" for the third time, *anchor* the feeling of relaxation by touching your thumb to your forefinger. The *click the pen* action becomes your physical cue for relaxation. Use this cue whenever you feel yourself getting tense. Simply touch your thumb to your forefinger and enjoy the feeling of relaxation that washes over you.

Konetta and me

I've found that it doesn't take very many repetitions to get this exercise to work. Shortly after discovering this technique, I put it to the test while hacking my mare, Konetta. We were riding down the road one morning and it happened to be trash day. Normally, trash day was not a big deal for her because she was accustomed to the garbage cans, but on this day, it was quite windy. As we walked down the road, we came upon a garbage can rolling straight toward us at a pretty good clip. Both of us got tight, and I thought, "I'm gonna die!" I clicked the pen a couple of times and immediately felt myself relax. As soon as I relaxed, Konetta became less concerned with the trash can, and we made it by safely. That convinced me of the effectiveness of this simple exercise.

3. In the third exercise, *squeeze the sponge,* you train yourself to relax by learning how to slow down your heart rate. You can do this by using the typical stress-and-recovery cycle that you experience during exercise. Go for a twenty-minute walk at a comfortable pace, and every few minutes increase your heart rate by walking faster or even jogging for ten to thirty seconds. You'll know you've increased your speed enough if you're breathing considerably harder, but you're not breathless. Each time you slow back down to the comfortable walk and feel your heart rate and breathing returning to normal, anchor this feeling by closing your hand gently in a fist as if you're squeezing water out of a sponge.

Cues for Anchoring Relaxation

Click the pen and *squeeze the sponge* are two of my favorite *anchors*, but, they certainly aren't the only ones available to you. Here are some other suggestions for cues. Pick the one that feels the most natural to you, or come up with one of your own.

- Touch your leg
- Clap your hands once
- Snap your fingers once
- Tap your fists together lightly
- Tug on your earlobe
- Touch the top of your head
- Rub your hands together

Once you've *anchored* the slowing of your heart rate with a specific cue, use that cue whenever you feel anxious. You'll be able to slow your heart rate on command because you've trained yourself to do so.

Essentials of Relaxation

- Use relaxation exercises to quiet your noisy *conscious* mind and get a "direct line" to your *subconscious* mind.
- You need to be relaxed in order to *visualize* effectively. Ideally, you want brain-wave activity to be in a low Alpha/borderline Theta state.
- The ideal for riding is a low Beta/borderline Alpha state.
- Take advantage of relaxation exercises to help you visualize more effectively as well as help you when riding. These exercises include *progressive relaxation, autogenics, sonic meditation, scanning, deep relaxation, belly breathing, plus/minus signs, the centaur, click the pen,* and *squeezing the sponge.*

10

Tension

Most riders suffer from tension from time to time. All sorts of things can make us tense. Occasionally, the tension is caused by stress from being in a new situation, such as riding in a clinic or at a show. Sometimes, your muscles get tight simply because you're trying too hard to be perfect. Often, the tension's roots are in fear—fear of the unknown, fear of getting injured, or fear of being embarrassed.

CASE HISTORY

Leigh

Learning how to relax is essential. Horses are so sensitive that if you're tense, you'll transmit your tension to your horse, and if he is tense, it's impossible to do quality work. He can only learn easily when he's relaxed. Also, if your muscles are tight, you won't be able to sit well and use your body effectively.

One of my students, Leigh, had to work through her tension.

Leigh had been a very skilled rider but, after an accident with a young horse, she was almost overwhelmed by fear-caused tension. She had been cantering a relatively young horse in an arena with a plastic chain around it. Her horse was startled and abruptly scooted sideways. Leigh wasn't at all unseated by this sudden movement, but his legs got tangled up in the plastic chain. Between the sound of the rattling chain and the feel of it around his legs, the young horse panicked and took off bucking pretty violently. The two of them parted company. Although Leigh was not hurt in the fall, she was really scared. In her mind, she linked cantering, bucking, young horses and plastic chains with extreme fright—a reaction that should be avoided at all costs. The experience was etched into her mind and she became overwhelmed by her tension and fear.

Her fear led her to come up with some interesting riding "rules." One of her rules was that she would not ride young horses—even if they were nicely started. Another rule: She would canter, but only very slowly. Her legs were saying "go," but her mind and heart were saying, "don't go too fast." She also wouldn't ride in any ring that had a plastic chain marking its perimeter.

In the effort to avoid the pain caused by being afraid, Leigh was actually creating a worse situation for herself. Tension now permeated every ride. Even though she had a reliable schoolmaster, she took a death grip on the reins if she thought he might be a little fresh. If she anticipated a buck because it was windy or the temperature had suddenly dropped, her entire body became rigid and tight. And, of course, she refused to ride in any arena with a chain around it. In fact, if she went to a horse show and the competition ring had such a barrier, she "scratched" her entry from classes.

Leigh's bad experience had caused her to link tense feelings to cantering.

Leigh knew she had to change this situation if she was ever going to really enjoy her riding. To help her, I reprogrammed her by going through the three steps of *getting the NAC*.

The first thing we did was *create leverage*. Leigh figured out why she absolutely *must* change: She *must* change because although she loved her horse, she spent much of her time in such a state of anxiety that she couldn't fully enjoy herself. She *must* change because her physical tension prevented her from riding effectively. She *must* change because she was humiliated when she scratched at shows and annoyed when she wasted entry-fee money.

Once Leigh realized that there was so much pain associated with *not* changing, she became committed to doing something about her situation.

First, she did some "homework" off her horse. I had her *visualize* a scene that made her tense, such as cantering down the long side of an arena surrounded by a plastic chain. As soon as her breathing got a little shallow—an indicator that she was getting anxious—we did an outrageous *pattern interrupt* by having her burp really loudly.

Then, we *reconditioned* and *reinforced* by linking a new empowering emotion to the situation by having her relive a time in her life when she felt adventurous and bold. She remembered the adrenaline rush she felt when she had gone rock climb-

ing. She built a new association by reliving the pleasurable memory of excitement and linking that feeling to the cantering scene. She repeated this association of excitement and cantering over and over again until it became conditioned. Once she had *reconditioned* herself, she *anchored* that feeling by using *buzzwords* like, "Geronimo!" or "Whoopee!"

After Leigh had done this homework without her horse, we had her *Get the NAC* while she was riding. When I could see her get tense, I'd break her mood with a *pattern interrupt* by saying something "off the wall" like, "Antonio Banderas called me last night and asked me out to dinner. Do you think I should go?" That got her mind off her fears, she giggled, and followed the *pattern interrupt* by repeating one of her *buzzwords.*

It only took a couple of weeks for Leigh to *recondition* and *reinforce* herself, and she now enjoys her riding so much more than she did when her ability was bound by a plastic chain! ✸

She reconditioned and reinforced by reliving the thrill of rock climbing in order to link a positive emotion to the canter.

Tension to Relaxation

- You can overcome fear and anxiety caused by a bad experience by *Getting the NAC.*

- Break a cycle of tension by *Getting the NAC*.

- *Anchor* a feeling of relaxation with emotional *buzzwords.*

11

The Impact of Self-Talk

Affirmations

In Chapter 7, I explained that *visualization* is the first way to change the programming—*change your software*—in your subconscious mind. The second way is through *self-talk*. Remember that your subconscious mind hears and believes everything you say, then sees the goal and goes for it. Be sure not to get "hung by your tongue!"

Now, I am going to look at a particular kind of self-talk called *empowering affirmations*, and later I'll explore additional ways you can use this method to *change your software*.

An *affirmation* is defined as a "positive assertion." An *affirmation* allows you to pick a quality thought and implant it into your subconscious mind. Just as with *visualization,* you need to know several things about *affirmations* in order to use them successfully to reprogram your mind.

Most importantly, you should phrase an *affirmation* in a positive way and in the present tense. (See *Positive Self-Talk* and *Keep it in the Present*, next.) In addition, you want to keep your *affirmation* brief so it will be easy to remember. Add emotion by using colorful words that stir you.[1]

I realize that it's going to sound strange to you when you word your *affirmation* in a positive way and in the present tense. You'll feel odd because you'll say something like, "I'm totally confident," or "I'm a calm and self-assured competitor," when that's just not the truth. Remember that the subconscious mind can't tell the difference between fact and fiction. It simply registers everything you say, positive or negative, and then tries to validate it.

Positive Self-Talk

Psychologists and neuroscientists have established that people carry on a continuous inner dialogue with themselves, sometimes up to three-hundred words a minute! In fact, you can't go more than eleven seconds without *"self-talking."*[2] Most *self-talk* is harmless. It's stuff like, "I need to go to the grocery store," "I think I'll wear my blue blouse tonight," or, "I should make an appointment for a haircut." Unfortunately, some of our inner dialogue is critical. When your self-talk is predominantly *negative*, you create the "mental software" for a particular belief to become a self-fulfilling prophecy. By innocently repeating that you always forget your test, you always have at least one knockdown when you jump, or you get really nervous in competition, you're creating the software to do just that!

You need to train yourself to use *positive self-talk* instead. As I mentioned before, the first reason to use *positive affirmations* is that there is no picture in the mind for the word "not." Avoiding the word "not" means you have to watch out for sneaky negatives, such as words with the contraction "n't." Saying you "don't" pull on the left rein is the same as saying you "do" pull on the left rein.

When I discussed *dominant thought* in Chapter 7, I explained that your subconscious mind cannot focus on the reverse of an idea—the second reason for phrasing your *affirmation* in a positive way. (If you tell yourself *not* to think about pink elephants all your mind gives you is pink elephants!) You will automatically move toward your *dominant thought* because your mind always moves you toward your thoughts—never away from them.

As far as your riding is concerned, you can't move *away* from impatience, *away* from sitting crookedly, or *away* from tension. You can only move *toward* patience, *toward* sitting straight or *toward* relaxation.

If you *tell* your mind not to think about pink elephants, all you see are pink elephants!

Keep It in the Present

Be sure to word your *affirmation* in the present tense. Rather than saying, "I will be focused at shows," or "I will sit straight and elegantly," say it in the present tense *as if* you already possess that quality. Of course, you are lying when you say, "I am focused at shows," and "I sit straight and elegantly," but the more you say it, the sooner it will become the truth. Remember, your subconscious mind programs and directs you as if you're a *guided missile*.

There is scientific documentation to support the idea that your *affirmations* don't have to be the truth in order for you to reprogram yourself. This evidence is presented in a theory, "The Theory of Cognitive Dissonance," first developed by Leon Festinger in 1957.

Festinger's theory says that if you hold two contradictory or opposing thoughts in your mind, you'll experience psychological dissonance which is felt as psychological tension. This state of tension drives you to reduce the conflict, much like hunger and thirst drive you to eat and drink. So, if you say "I'm relaxed when I compete," but in reality, you know you're a nervous wreck, this creates a conflict in your subconscious mind. In order to reduce the discomfort of the opposing messages, the subconscious will do everything in its power to create the most recently imposed *affirmation*. This is why it doesn't matter if your new *affirmation* is a lie or not: If you repeat it often enough, it will eventually override your old negative thoughts.[3]

Punch Up Your Affirmations

Language is so powerful that you can change how you feel simply by changing one or two words. In Chapter 13, *Visualization—Refining the Technique*, I'll explain how and why it's important to add *emotion* to your *mental* pictures. For now, just understand that your *verbal* pictures—your *affirmations*—will also be more intense. Notice how the following statements make you feel:

I'm happy.	I'm ecstatic.
I'm calm.	I'm cool as a cucumber.
I'm athletic.	I'm an elite athlete.

I'm a good rider.	I'm a warrior athlete.
I want to learn this skill.	I'm absolutely committed to mastering this skill.
I'm a good competitor.	I'm a savvy competitor.
I'm patient.	I'm endlessly patient.
I want to be a better rider.	I'm passionate about becoming a brilliant rider.
I always work hard at improving.	I'm totally committed to excelling.
I'm prepared to ride cross-country.	I'm a masterful, dynamic, cross-country rider.
I'm determined to reach my goals.	I'm unstoppable.
I'm having a great ride.	I'm having an outstanding ride.

You should not only use words that stir you, but when you say your *affirmation*, really feel it. Be a DQ. (A "drama queen", not a "dressage queen"!) Say the *affirmation* with intensity and absolute conviction, *as if* you already possess the quality you want. Doing so engages your entire nervous system.[4]

Say It Often and Say It Out Loud

I sit the trot with ease.

Remember that with both *affirmations* and mental pictures, reprogramming your mind is a numbers game. If you've said to yourself ten thousand times, "I can't sit the trot very well." Then you need to say to yourself, ten thousand and one times. "I sit the trot as if I'm part of my horse."

It's fairly easy to rack up those numbers. Simply repeat your affirmation any-time throughout your day. Pair it with other activities that are part of your daily routine. Say it aloud when you're driving to work, when you're taking a shower, while you're preparing dinner, or when you're grooming your horse.

Saying your *affirmation* out loud works because you're involving two more of your senses—*auditory* and *kinesthetic*. As you inhale, *think* your *affirmation*. As you exhale, *feel* it as you say it aloud. The rationale behind this approach is that as you inhale and think your *affirmation*, you're owning it and taking it into your total being. As you exhale and say it aloud, you're rewiring your brain.[5]

Buzzwords

In Chapter 3, I introduced you to using *buzzwords* when I discussed *anchors*. Now, I'll elaborate on this amazingly simple and incredibly effective way to get yourself into the right state for peak performance. Choose words that are positive and full of emotion, because your *buzzword* signals your brain and body to do what you have to do. If you're distracted at a show, say, "Focus!" If you're ready to leave the start box to tackle the cross-country course at a horse trial, say, "Charge!" If you're riding a dressage test, say, "Smooth." If you're timid about jumping a particular fence, say "Bold."

CASE HISTORY

Robin

Here's an example of how Robin Clark used *buzzwords* to bolster her self-confidence. She wrote:

"In 2000, as I began competing my dear Thoroughbred, Bailey, at low-level horse trials, I picked up a copy of your book, *That Winning Feeling!* I had already read some of your other technical books and found them helpful—I still do. I am a novice, adult rider, middle of age yet young of heart. I had competed a schoolhorse previously, but never my own green horse. We were well prepared, but I was nervous due to his inexperience jumping—particularly the fact that we never took a straight line to the fence. He was more like a worm meandering back and forth. This was a real challenge for me! I liked

Implant positive thoughts in your subconscious by repeating them out loud throughout your day.

Robin Clark
with Bailey

your idea regarding writing *buzzwords* on index cards. My *buzz-words* were:

CONFIDENT
FORWARD
STRAIGHT (Please God, to the fence!)
ORGANIZED

"I kept my index card in my car—a traveling card, actually. It went in my office on my desk and, yes, to the horse trials with me. I taped it to the chair near my horse's stall so it was always in my field of vision. Some people thought it was hilarious and teased me. They were not laughing when we consistently placed in the top three all year. I would repeat my little litany over and over to myself, and to Bailey... 'We are *confident*, we are *forward*, we are *straight*, and *organized*,' and relatively speaking, you know, we really were! We were the Adult Green-As-Grass Hi-Point Champions for the Greater Houston Combined Training Association that year. Preparation and hard work do pay off especially when you add equal parts of confidence!

"Bailey is my reflection and I am his on an emotional and psychological level—if I think we can, so does he, and vice versa. Thanks for showing me that with a positive attitude, 'I *can*,' can be my reality.

"By the way, God does have a sense of humor. The person who had the most sarcastic attitude the day of that first show was embarrassed by being thrown ungracefully at the water jump. Dripping wet, she asked if she could borrow my index card for the next horse trial!"

Changing Yourself from the Inside Out

I find it amazing how simply repeating a word over and over again can have a profound effect. On the one hand, saying a word such as "confident," "elegant," or "poised," will be reflected in your outward appearance. By the same token, repeating a negative word like "depressed," "discouraged," "afraid," or "nervous," takes its toll on the way you appear.

A good example of this was a woman I met at one of my seminars. This woman told me how she used a *buzzword* to *change herself from the inside out*. She happened to be a little on the "chunky" side and didn't have the ideal rider's body. She explained that she had a real challenge seeing herself as an elegant rider.

She was at a competition and decided to pick a powerful word to see if she could change the way she felt about herself and, therefore, how she rode. The word she chose was "graceful." Throughout her ride, she repeated "graceful" to herself. When she finished, she felt pretty good about herself. But she was totally dumbfounded when a friend came up to her and said, "Wow! That was wonderful! You looked so graceful. It was like watching a dance."

You can also *change yourself from the inside out* by changing the words you use to define a situation.

Try this out. The next time someone asks you how you're feeling, instead of automatically saying "Fine," say "Outstanding!" and see how your body responds. Or, the next time you have a disappointing go at a show, instead of saying your ride was terrible, say, "My horse tried so hard! I'm really proud of him." I'm willing to bet that those words will make you feel a whole lot better.

The Power of Words

Once you understand the *power of words*, using *empowering affirmations* and *buzzwords* will become a part of your life. One rider explained how she used them to help her get what she wanted in competition. She wrote:

"Prior to my first event of the season, I learned my test by visualizing it over and over again. Considering we pay to compete, it seems ironic that we all get so nervous about doing something we really want to do. I am no exception, so I decided to work on my show nerves by using the following affirmations. I repeatedly told myself, 'I love to compete. I am cool and collected in competitions. I love my sport.' Amazingly, I really enjoyed myself. Someone even commented on how calm I was!

"The other incredible thing was that I kept telling myself that I was going to get 7's and 8's [out of 10] on my dressage test. Well, the majority of my marks were 7's and 8's!"

Throughout the years, I've also had some incredible things happen to me that illustrate the *power of words*. I don't know why it still surprises me that it works the way it does, but, I know I'm always delighted and amazed when I "claim" something, and eventually it becomes a reality.

I remember one remarkable example that happened early on in my competitive career. That year, I had a great season showing a young horse. I had so much fun that when the shows ended, I proclaimed, "Next year I'm going to compete two horses, and one of them will be at FEI (Federation Equestrian International) levels." FEI levels are the most advanced international tests, and I had no money to buy such a horse, but I just kept repeating those words all winter long. In April, a very inexpensive, older horse that was trained to the FEI levels came on the market, and I thought, 'This is it!" I was dumbfounded when someone bought him before I even had a chance to try him. The spring shows were nearly underway, and I couldn't believe my FEI horse had just slipped through my fingers.

Nevertheless, I kept repeating my mantra, "I'm going to show two horses, and one of them is going to be an FEI horse." Then, out of the blue, two weeks before the first show, another horse became available, and I was even able to find a sponsor who would help me with his expenses.

So, sure enough, when I went to that first competition in June, I campaigned two horses—one an FEI horse. It made me a firm believer that "what you say is what you get."

Another startling example of the *power of words* occurred after I had ridden a season with the great dressage trainer, Herbert Rehbein, at his establishment Grohnwoldhof, in Germany. Training with Rehbein was a most worthwhile experience, but also a very expensive venture. I knew that if my horse, Zapatero, and I were going to be taken seriously, I needed to go to Europe more than once. My plan was to return to Europe the following year not only to train, but also to compete.

I had calculated that the return trip would cost approximately thirty thousand dollars. So, I started chanting out loud, "Thirty thousand dollars, thirty thousand dollars." I'd be grooming my horse to the tune of, "Thirty thousand dollars, thirty thousand dollars." I'd be walking him on a loose rein saying, "Thirty thousand dollars, thirty thousand dollars." I'd drive my car down the road saying, "Thirty thousand dollars, thirty thousand dollars." I programmed myself like this for a couple of months.

Almost immediately after I returned home from Europe, I had to prepare for the National Championships at the United States Equestrian Team (USET) headquarters in Gladstone, New Jersey. Fortunately, the competition was a huge success. Even though Zapatero was still a fairly green Grand Prix horse, we did very well and ended up placing third. Shortly after the awards were given, I was thrilled to discover that the United States Olympic Committee was going to award three training grants to the top three horses so they could go to Europe. Guess how much the grant was for? You got it! Thirty thousand dollars!

Essentials of Self-Talk

* Change your *mental software* with *empowering affirmations.*
* Word *affirmations* in a positive way and in the present tense.
* Keep *affirmations* brief.
* Punch up your *affirmations* with colorful language.
* Repeat *affirmations* often and out loud.
* "The Theory of Cognitive Dissonance" states that if you hold two opposing thoughts in your mind, your subconscious will attempt to reduce the tension from your conflicting feelings by making the most recent *affirmation* come true.
* Use *buzzwords* to get yourself in the right state for peak performance.
* Use *buzzwords* to *change yourself from the inside out.*
* Believe in the *power of words.*

12
Doubt

oubt goes hand in hand with insecurity. Once again, I think it's just part of the human condition for us to question our ability, talent, and skill. However, when you're overwhelmed by doubt, you can become paralyzed. If you don't believe in yourself, chances are you'll become passive and ineffective. You're not going to be able to train your horse very well if you question yourself every step of the way. Your horse needs you to ride with authority.

It's bad enough not to believe in yourself, but if you also doubt your horse, you transmit that to him. Imagine the subtle signals you give when you canter down to a triple combination and your self-talk and body language say to your horse, "This is a tricky distance. I don't think you're clever enough to handle it."

On the other hand, believing in your horse can allow him to perform far beyond his innate talent. When I rode Zapatero, the alternate for the 1992 Olympic team, I certainly thought of him as a very special horse. But now that some time has passed and I can be more objective, I wouldn't call him a world-beater. At that time, in my mind, however, he was "the best horse in the world." I had blind faith in his ability and he ended up being among the best of the best. The truth was that much of what we accomplished had less to do with his innate talent and more to do with my unconditional belief in him.

Belief

Just what is belief? A belief is a feeling of certainty about what something means.

Your current level of skill, as well as what you accomplish in the future, is going to be determined by what you believe about yourself and about your horse. Unfortunately, more often than not, we come up with limiting beliefs that prevent us from becoming better riders. Some common ones are:

I'm not very good because:

☞ I started as an adult.

☞ I'm timid.

☞ I don't have enough time to practice.

☞ I'm not fit enough.

☞ I'm a nervous competitor.

☞ I'm just an amateur.

☞ I always have a rail down in show jumping.

☞ I get claustrophobic when all the horses are in a pack at the start of my endurance ride.

Know that you can change and create the reality you desire for yourself. This process may involve little more than simply *deciding* to change by choosing new beliefs that will help make you the rider you'd like to be.

Magnetic Belief Screen

Psychologist Lee Pulos, author of *The Power of Visualization*, explains that when we say that we want something that conflicts with our subconscious beliefs about ourselves, the subconscious belief always prevails. He suggests a great exercise to help free ourselves from our limiting beliefs. It's called the *Magnetic Belief Screen*.

You can build a *magnetic belief screen* in your mind by imagining a large door—about seven-feet tall and five-feet wide. A fine, gold-mesh screen is stretched across the entire doorway, from top to bottom and side to side. Across the top, there is a sign that reads in large print, *Magnetic Belief Screen*.

Once you can picture this screen in your mind's eye, see yourself stepping slowly through it several times. The screen filters out all your negative, limiting beliefs. They remain behind as residue on the screen like lint from the screen in your clothes dryer.

Denny Emerson and I talked about how important it is to believe in yourself. The belief you have in yourself has to be so complete that you know you can be successful even when the facts say otherwise. Denny's career is a perfect example of succeeding in spite of having the odds stacked against him. He explained:

"I saw my first event in 1961 at Groton House, South Hamilton, Massachusetts. That day, I decided that I would be on the United States Equestrian Team. I made that decision with nothing real to base it on. I was twenty, and I had never jumped a fence. I had no money, no lessons, no expertise. I just believed in myself and committed myself to my goal.

As you visualize stepping through the screen, all your limiting, negative beliefs are left behind like residue on the lint trap in your clothes dryer.

"At the time, I was in my senior year at Dartmouth, and I had been doing the sport for about a year. I thought, 'How am I going to learn how to do this? If I'm going to be on the team, I'm obviously going to need money. Plus, my horse is green and we both have a lot to learn.' So, I got a job teaching at Far Hills Country Day School in New Jersey, because that's where the USET was located. I figured if I was going to learn how to do this sport, I better go watch people who knew what they were doing.

"My belief in myself and my commitment to my goal was so complete that at age twenty-two, I'd go down at night on my green, Preliminary horse and with no help at all, I'd jump all the advanced fences just to prove that I could do it.

"Because I believed in myself, it wasn't a great surprise to me when I got my gold medal at the World Championships. I knew I was going to do it. How did I

know? I just made a conscious choice. I just decided that I was going to."

Denny said believing in yourself should extend to the point of even having *heroic daydreams*. He then told me a story he had read about Kim Vinoski Severson, member of the gold medal Three-Day Event team at the World Equestrian Games in Jerez, Spain in 2002. He said:

"Kim's six years old. She's galloping around on her pony. Suddenly, she stops and acknowledges an imaginary audience. When asked, 'What are you doing?,' she says, 'I'm waving to the cheering crowd.'"

"In Kim's mind, she was watching a *preview of coming attractions*. She had a vision of what she would achieve and twenty years later, she made it happen."

I told Denny I could relate to Kim's story. In the years that I was competing Zapatero, I would jog near my home in Vermont as part of my own fitness routine. As I approached my house toward the end of my run, I'd always look at the flagpole in my front yard. I'd visualize an American flag slowly being raised and I'd hear the proud strains of the national anthem in my mind. The image was so vivid that by the time I reached my house, I always had tears in my eyes.

Kim Vinoski Severson on Winsome Adante at the
World Equestrian Games at Jerez de la Frontera, Spain, in 2002

In order to achieve your goals, unconditional belief in your horse is just as important as unconditional belief in yourself.

My friend Susan Blinks, member of the bronze-medal-winning Olympic dressage team in Sydney in 2000, is another champion who always believes in the horses she trains. I could tell you about any one of many horses I've seen Sue train over the years, but I've chosen Delano, because I am personally very fond of him.

Sue brought Delano over from Holland as a six-year-old. He was a lovely, dark brown horse with expressive movement. "D's" strengths were that, he was a bottomless pit in terms of energy, had fabulous, expressive movement, and was a real eager-to-please type.

Unfortunately, "D" also had one glaring weakness. He was a very sensitive soul who had a lot of "skeletons" in his closet. Sue explained, "Delano was an over-achiever at heart. Because he was so physically talented and tried so hard, his original trainers rushed him. He was asked to do work he wasn't ready to do. When he couldn't do it, either because the proper foundation hadn't been laid or he wasn't strong enough, his riders got aggressive with him. This made him 'nuts,' because he was already doing his very best. He became overwhelmed and would act out by biting his own chest, climbing the arena walls, or hysterically skittering away in an attempt to leave the ring."

"D" was so emotionally scarred that any number of things could trigger a panic attack. He might be confused by a new exercise. He might be trying too hard and worried that he wasn't doing the right thing. Or, he might be at a horse show where the atmosphere was electric, or competing at night under lights.

Sue Blinks on Delano; with Flim Flam

Because he was so emotional, Sue often met trainers and clinicians who had a negative attitude toward Delano. They'd ask, "Why do you bother with this horse? He'll never be more than a Prix St. Georges schoolhorse." But, Sue loved and believed in "D." She felt he had the ability to do the difficult movements well. Plus, she knew she could always count on him to try his heart out. She felt that he just needed to learn to trust her, and she was willing to give him the time to make it work.

Sue went on, "The problem was that his previous trainers had tried to teach him words without teaching him the alphabet first. This left him confused and panicked. I taught him the alphabet before I put letters together to form words. This slow approach allowed me to build a base of trust, and then gradually I could push him more and more. Slowly but surely, he realized he could do things without being overfaced."

In time, Sue's belief in Delano paid off. In 1995, he was the United States Dressage Federation Intermediare II Horse of the Year, and placed third at the National Finals in Gladstone, New Jersey. He culminated his career as a Grand Prix horse by being named the alternate horse for the 1998 World Equestrian Games in Rome.

Betsy Steiner and Rainier

Role Playing

When I'm struggling to assume a quality I desire such as poise or confidence, I find that the struggle is often rooted in my self-doubt. My limiting beliefs prevent me from riding to my potential. In order to overcome those limiting beliefs, I do a lot of *role-playing*. By pretending I'm a rider who possesses the quality I believe I lack, I'm able to act *as if* that quality is mine. Since I'm not Jane Savoie anymore—with all of my shortcomings and issues—I can reach a higher standard.

Here are two examples of how I've used *role-playing* to act *as if* I'm someone else and thus, ride better.

I often use *role-playing* when I'm having one of my "klutzy" days. Those are the kind of days when I feel so uncoordinated that I can't use my left leg without my right foot falling out of the stirrup. I'm so overwhelmed by my lack of talent that I want to quit.

Isabel Werth riding Nissan Gigolo

On days like this, I pretend I'm Betsy Steiner, member of the U.S. World Championship dressage team in Sweden in 1990, and author of *A Gymnastic Riding System Using Mind, Body, and Spirit.* Betsy is one of those riders who seems to have absolute control over her elegant position at all times. I doubt she ever has a spastic, bumbling day. So on my bad days, I do my Betsy imitation and before you know it, I ride like a world champion!

When I'm consumed with doubt at competitions, I use *role-playing* as well. In the past, when I found myself competing alongside the top riders in the world, I started to doubt myself, and a little insecure voice inside said, "You have no business being in this company. You don't belong here."

On days like this, I pretend I'm 1996 Olympic individual gold medalist, Isabel Werth, from Germany. Isabel is a true competitor. When the chips are down, she always rises to the occasion.

In order to give you a little insight into her character, I'll tell you of an incident that took place at the European Dressage Championships in Donaueschingen, Germany in 1991. Isabel was just about ready to leave the warm-up area and enter the competition arena when her coach, Dr. Uwe Schulten-Baumer said to her, " You should have seen Nicole and Rembrant's ride. It was unbelievable!"

Germany's Nicole Uphoff, Olympic individual gold medalist in Seoul (1988) and Barcelona (1992), and Isabel had dominated the sport of dressage for several years and were longtime rivals. The two of them often vied for the top spot at international competitions. They are both extremely gifted and on any given day, either one of them could be placed atop the scoreboard.

If my coach said what Schulten-Baumer said to Isabel moments before I was to compete, I probably would have crumbled and thought, "Well, I might as well go back to the barn, right now! What's the use? No one is going to top that score."

But Isabel, the warrior athlete, responded to her coach with, "Oh yeah! Well, just watch this!" and she cantered determinedly and purposefully into the ring. Rather than being mentally defeated, her belief in herself made her ride better, harder, and more expressively, and she ended up winning the gold medal, beating her rival by almost seventeen points, a very significant lead in dressage competition.

Doubt to Belief

TIPS FOR CHANGE

- Turn *doubt* into *belief* by making a *magnetic belief screen* and filter out your limiting beliefs.
- Create the reality you want simply by changing your beliefs about yourself and your horse.
- Have *heroic daydreams.*
- Use *role-playing* to overcome your self-imposed limitations.

13

Visualization—Refining the Technique

Five Ingredients for Effective Visualization

Perhaps you've dabbled with *visualization* to improve your riding but abandoned it because you didn't get the results you wanted. Let's examine your technique. You might be missing one little ingredient that could make all the difference in the world.

In order to use visualization effectively, you need to do five things:

1. Make your images vivid by *filling in details*.
2. Involve as many of your *five senses* as possible.
3. Include *emotion* in your mental picture.
4. Do your imaging when you're *relaxed*.
5. *Repeat* your images regularly.

When you fill in details, you make your mental pictures even more vivid and, therefore, increase the likelihood of a successful outcome.

Let's say you've decided to use visualization to improve your horse's trot extensions but you don't seem to be having much success. Maybe the problem is simply that your images are too sketchy. For example, maybe you picture your horse coming through the short side of the ring. You give a half-halt in the corner. As you leave the corner and start down the long side of the ring, you close your calves to ask for the extension. You "see" your horse power himself down the long side as he lengthens his frame and his stride. You repeat this image over and over again.

Make your images more effective by filling in the details.

That's a good starting point, but unfortunately, this image isn't detailed enough to really help you. In order to improve these trot extensions, you need to make the picture much more colorful by filling in details.

Start by picturing your horse. He's a 16.1 hand bay gelding with a small star on his forehead. He has two small white socks on his front ankles. He's wearing white boots on all four legs. And, what are you wearing? You have on your navy breeches, black boots, beige polo shirt, gloves with crochet on the back, and your helmet with the worn velvet on one side.

Now what kind of day is it? It's a beautiful spring day. The temperature is about seventy degrees. There's not a cloud in the sky. There's no humidity and no bugs! There's a gentle breeze wafting by your face.

Where are you? You're in the ring at your stable. The footing is a mixture of sand and rubber. It feels very alive and springy.

With that much detail, you're off to a good start. To really get some "bang for your buck," however, make the image even more vivid by involving as many of your five senses as possible.

Involve Your Senses

Neuroscientists at the University of California have used a radioactive imaging technique, called Petscan, to look at brain activity during problem solving activities. Their research shows that when the five senses—sight, touch, hearing, smell, and taste—are used during visualization, the wiring of the brain actually becomes denser; specifically, brain cells develop thicker stems (axons), and the connections between the cells become more complex (synapses). When you use all of your senses you essentially increase the density of the wiring in your brain, and your mental programming becomes much more powerful.[1]

I'd like you to try a simple exercise so you can see the value in adding your five senses to your imaging. Imagine that you're holding a lemon. *Look* at the lemon. *Feel* the size and shape of it as well as the texture of the rind as you turn it over in your hand a few times. Now, take this imaginary lemon and place it down on a table. Pick up a knife and cut it in half. *Listen* to the sound of the knife piercing the rind and slicing through the juicy pulp. Bring half of the lemon up to your nose and *smell* that lemony, fresh fragrance. Squeeze the lemon and *hear* it "squoosh" as you *feel* the juice trickle down between your fingers and down your arm. Then bring that half of the lemon back up to your mouth and take a nice, big bite. Crruuuunnnnchhhhhh!

Do you feel anything inside your mouth? Are you salivating? Do your lips pucker? If you let yourself experience the imaginary lemon with all five senses, you're bound to notice some sort of physiological reaction. Don't you find it amazing that you can create a very real reaction inside your mouth to something that exists only in your imagination?

Now that you've experienced how powerful it is to involve your five senses in your mental pictures, let's continue with our image of the trot extension. But this time, involve your senses.

See your horse's neck in front of you. Notice how his ears move back and forth as he listens attentively to you.

Feel the width of your horse's body underneath you and a firm, but elastic rein contact.

Smell the fly spray, the dressing you've used on your tack, the flowers in bloom, the clean air on a crisp spring day.

Taste the salt from your sweat.

Hear the regularity of the footfalls at the trot. One-two-one-two.

See yourself riding in collected trot through the second corner of the short side of the ring and giving a half-halt to coil the spring of the hind legs. You don't even need to close your legs to ask for the extension as you come out of the corner. There is so much compressed power within your horse's body, all you have to do is soften your hands a bit and he surges forward.

See your horse lengthening his stride and frame, yet notice how his balance feels uphill—like an airplane taking off or a speedboat in the water. Then zero in on his hind legs. Exaggerate the image. *See* his hind legs bending and engaging to such a degree that they practically hit his belly with each stride.

Exaggerate the image of an extension by "seeing" your horse: coil his hind legs, take off like a speedboat, hit his belly with his hooves, and recompress like an accordian.

At the end of the ring, all you have to do to come back to the collected trot is close your outside hand in a fist. Your horse is so attentive that he responds immediately by compressing his body like an accordion.

Throughout the entire exercise—the collected trot, the extended trot, and back to the collected trot—you *hear* the rhythm and the tempo of the footfalls remaining exactly the same—one-two-one-two.

We're not done yet. We can do even more to make this image vivid by adding emotion.

Get Emotional

Most people are familiar with the idea that we have two brains in one—the left and the right. The left brain operates from *intelligence*. It's the logical, analytical, linear, verbal part of the brain. The right brain operates from *intuition*—the non-verbal creative, musical, emotional, pattern-seeing part of the brain.

When we project emotion into our image, we mobilize a third brain structure—the limbic system or mid-brain. In fact, the ideal state for visualizing is a combination of your logical left brain, your creative right brain, and your emotional midbrain. This combination sets the stage for effective visualization, bringing more of your brain into play and adding more energy to your mental pictures.[2]

Add *emotion* to your image by seeing yourself fly across the diagonal with wild abandon!

How can you can add emotion to your image of the extension? Experience a sense of harmony and "oneness." Feel as if you and your horse are so in tune with each other that your horse's body is your body. You're so much a part of each other, it's hard to tell where you leave off and he begins.

Perhaps you have "control" issues, and the idea of a huge extension intimidates you. In that case, the emotions you'll want to feel are *boldness*, *excitement*, and *freedom*. Fly across the diagonal with wild abandon.

Maybe your horse looks so breathtaking that you well up with *pride* as you watch him "sail" magnificently down the long side with his feet barely touching the ground.

There you have it. You've now created a very

vivid image of an extension. You've filled in details, involved as many of your senses as possible, and included emotion. There are actually two more things that you should do: First, practice your imaging when you're in as *relaxed* a state as possible. Second, *repeat* your images on a regular basis.

Relaxation

In Chapter 9, I gave you a number of relaxation exercises. If you've already begun using *progressive relaxation* or *autogenics*, you can simply sit in a chair, close your eyes, take a deep breath, and as you exhale, say your *buzzwords*. I offered examples like, "Let go," "Relax," and "I am calm."

If you haven't *anchored* a feeling of relaxation with a word or phrase, the simplest way for you to relax is to do some *belly breathing*. Take in a deep breath until you feel your stomach expand. As you exhale, feel yourself lowering down into the chair. Repeat this a second time. Then, inhale for the third time but this time hold your breath for ten seconds. Once again, as you exhale, let your body become heavier as it sinks down deeper into the chair.

Once you've taken your three *belly breaths*, you're ready to begin your imaging session.

Repetition

For maximum results, *repeat* your mental rehearsal on a regular schedule. Do it at least once a day. I've found that the best time of day is when I first wake-up, or just before I fall asleep. My chattering, conscious mind is most quiet at those times, and I can *change the software* in my subconscious mind more easily.

Time Frame for Change

Once you've started visualizing, you'll gradually start to notice changes and improvements in your riding. How quickly those changes occur depends on how many repetitions you need to do in order to override your old negative beliefs. Remember, if there's something you don't like about your riding, you've probably repeated that negative image thousands of times. You need to run your new program all those thousands, plus one.

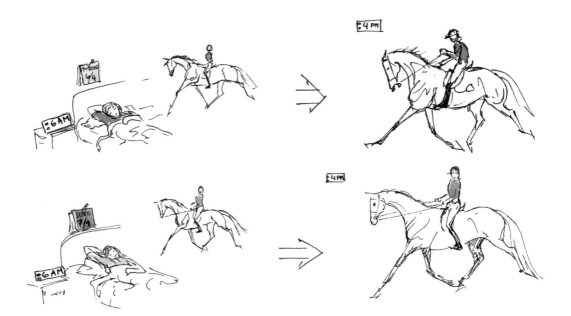

Remember, just because you haven't noticed change doesn't mean you aren't on the road to improving. You need to run your new program enough times to eventually override the old one.

Don't give up because you don't sense any improvement. Maybe you've only repeated the new image nine hundred and ninety-nine times. You're so close to making the changes you want, all you need to do is practice two more times in order to make your new program stronger than the old one. Hang in there!

More Essentials of Visualization

- For effective visualization:
  1. Fill in *details.*
  2. Involve your five *senses.*
  3. Get *emotional.*
  4. Visualize when you're *relaxed.*
  5. *Repeat* your mental pictures regularly.
- Don't give up. You need to repeat your images often enough to override your old, negative software.

I n order to fulfill your potential as a rider, you need to be confident. There's a huge difference, however, between being confident and being arrogant. Arrogance can really get in the way, not only of your education, but also of developing a respectful relationship with your horse.

For some people, I think arrogance is part of youthful self-assuredness that makes them feel invincible. For others, arrogance is simply an expression of insecurity. The arrogant rider covers up her insecurity by acting all-knowing. Because she knows it all and thinks her way is the only way, she closes herself off from all sorts of chances to become more educated.

The opposite of arrogance is humility. Humility is a huge part of the equation

The difference between domination and submission is the difference between a miserable horse and a happy one.

Sylvia Loch with Palomo

to becoming a better horseman. If you're ever going to really form a partnership with your horse based on mutual respect, you need to be humble enough to listen to him and respond to his fears, needs, and challenges.

Sadly, the arrogant rider's horse is obedient only because he's been dominated, while the humble rider's horse is obedient because he is willingly submissive. The difference between *domination* of a "groveling," subservient horse, and *submissiveness* of a forward, willing partner, is also the difference between a miserable horse and a happy horse.

Using your horse to show off and bring prestige and the status that goes with it to yourself is another pitfall of arrogance.

Sylvia Loch, author of *The Art of Classical Riding*, *The Classical Seat*, and *The Classical Rider* agrees. She says, "It's no good trying to show what a good rider you are. The whole thing is to show how wonderful your horse is. We are merely the medium for his brilliant brush strokes of color." Sylvia then illustrates her point with a story about one of her favorite horses, Palomo Lunares, a very old Portuguese, Lusitano/Arabian schoolmaster. "I bought him when he was fourteen and cast out into a field as a retired bullfighting stallion. Palomo had a pretty onerous lifestyle before coming into my possession. All of his work had been concentrated on his athleticism, turning skills, and boldness. He was thus clearly afraid to relax.

When Palomo came to me, I spent two years just trying to teach him to relax and enjoy hacking out without him jogging and piaffing and thinking that he had to perform all the time. Now that he has been cured of his anxiety and has learned to develop a real relationship and to show love, Palomo is absolutely splendid to ride, and he loves to show off his movements in front of an audience in a public setting and to help students at home. However, if occasionally, thoughts enter my head such as, 'Don't we look good together,' things can go wrong. I simply have to throw away all sense of ego when riding him—he is there to help me teach, and to show other people how horses like to be ridden. He is not interested in competitive glory, and I have never competed him. He is my greatest schoolmaster."

One of the other trainers I admire for his humility is a cowboy from Montana, Curt Pate. Among the many things I appreciate about Curt is his readiness to admit how arrogant he was in his youth. His openness has allowed him to develop into a top horseman who continues to grow as he learns both from his animals and experts in all riding disciplines.

Curt told me how he's changed over the years. He said:

"When I was younger, I was pretty rough on horses. When I was right in the middle of it—yanking, whipping, and spurring—it was all about me, never about the horse.

"I didn't feel good about being so rough, but I grew up that way. Everyone was doing it, so I did too, but I knew it wasn't right. You see, I'm an animal lover. I don't even like to hunt. When I was growing up, we had a slaughterhouse. I just couldn't do the killing. I'd rather do the two worst jobs—hauling guts and salting hides—than do the killing.

"Even today, when I see people who are rough and cruel with their horses, I can hardly watch. I got to thinking about it, and I realize it's because the roughness reminds me of when I was in that stage. I'm upset that I had to go through it to get to another phase. But I understand that this is just part of becoming a better trainer. You don't know what's good until you've seen a little bit of what's bad.

"Being aggressive is fine if you're a boxer or a skier. But we have living, breathing, feeling animals underneath us. I don't think it's right for us to use them as a stepping-stone to get to the next level. "I finally came to the conclusion that it's wrong to intrude on another creature's life, ruining its day just to make ours better. That realization marked a big change for me in my approach to training."

One of Curt's favorite stories is how he was humbled by a mare that was brought to one of his colt-starting clinics. Curt explained:

"This mare was a real problem. She absolutely refused to move forward in the round pen. She would kick at you, run backward, and urinate. I finally just got on the horse. All she would do was buck, and squeal, and pee. Here I was 'the big

Curt Pate

horse trainer,' and I just couldn't get her to go forward."

Curt decided to train the mare for a month, thinking he'd figure out some way to reach this horse. But the solution didn't come from him, he said.

"I turned her out with a bunch of colts. It was so strange. For awhile, she just stayed by herself and wouldn't even go with the other horses to eat. It was really hot at that time, and there were lots of flies around. All the colts were huddled together to fight the flies. Eventually, the flies drove her crazy, and she went over and got in with the group. That was a huge turning point for her. From then on, she became a horse. She's actually wonderful now, and her owner thoroughly enjoys trail riding her.

"I have to laugh because here I was, being the clever horse trainer and thinking I had to do all sorts of things to get her going, when the problem was that she just didn't know how to be a horse. I wasn't able to change her, but a pesky fly was responsible for her transformation!"

One of the other characteristics that underscores Curt's humility is the value he places on education.

"If I have a house or a car, those things can be taken away or stolen from me. But knowledge in my head is the one thing that no one can take away. Of course, I can take it away if I let myself get stagnant. That's why I keep trying to refresh myself and see things differently.

"My whole mission in life is to become a better hand. So, I watch the experts in other disciplines and try to figure out how I can use their expertise to make me a better cowboy. I'll ask myself how I can use what they do to fit my situation. For example, I figure my cow horses are kind of endurance horses because they have to stay fit and sound as they travel twenty miles a day. So, I study endurance riders. Then I think that my horses are kind of event horses because they have to go over logs and down through creeks. So, I watch event riders. I even think my horses are kind of dressage horses because they have to make some of the same maneuvers that dressage horses do. So, I study dressage riders. Even when I'm working at a Horse Expo, I try to watch as much as I can. I always ask myself what I learned and how much better of a horseman I've become as a result. That's how I judge if I've had a good day."

Arrogance to Humility

TIPS FOR CHANGE

- There's a world of difference between confidence and arrogance.
- To become a better horseman, you need to turn arrogance into humility.
- The humble rider listens to her horse, and is responsive to his fears, needs and challenges.
- The humble rider doesn't use her horse to show off or gain status.
- The humble rider places a huge value on education and is open to new ideas and approaches.

15

Attitude Is Everything

Your Attitude, Not Your Aptitude, Determines Your Altitude

Here's a radical thought: How far you go in life—whether in riding, your career, fitness goals, other sports, or personal relationships—has very little to do with how clever or talented you are, or how much money you have. The single biggest factor in your success is your attitude.

The idea that your *attitude, not your aptitude determines your altitude* isn't something I've arbitrarily come up with. As a matter of fact, some years back, a study was done that determined that eighty-five percent of the reason that people are successful and earn accomplishments, promotions, and awards in their work is because of their attitude, and only fifteen percent has to do with technical expertise.[1] The fact that attitude plays such a huge role in success is exciting news. It's empowering because although we might not be able to control the hand that we're dealt, we do have absolute control over how we're going to react to that hand.

Perhaps Abraham Lincoln summed it up best when he said that most people are about as happy as they make up their minds to be. Decide to be happy. Choose to have the right attitude. Since it's your attitude not your talent, skill, or wealth that determines your success, preserve a *winning attitude* at all costs.

Choose a Winning Attitude

When I'm in Florida, I always enjoy watching one particular television commercial

To control your destiny, play on the one string you have available: your attitude.

for a well-known local insurance company. It features a ninety-four-year-old woman who has a *winning attitude*. She says, with a twinkle in her eye, "When I wake up every morning, I have two choices. I can choose to be happy or I can choose to be sad. I choose to be happy."

Michael Page, three-time Olympic Three-Day Event rider, recognizes the importance of choosing a *winning attitude*. In a speech at a conference for the American Riding Instructors Certification Program he said:

"The longer I live, the more I realize the impact of attitude on life. Attitude, to me, is more important than facts. It is more important than the past, than education, than money, than circumstances, than failures, than successes, than what other people think, or say or do. It is more important than appearance, giftedness, or skill. It will make or break a company...a church...a home. The remarkable thing is we have a choice everyday regarding the attitude we will embrace for that day. We cannot change our past...we cannot change the fact that people will act in a certain way. We cannot change the inevitable. The only thing we can do is play on the one string we have, and that is our attitude...I am convinced that life is ten percent what happens to me and ninety percent how I react to it. And, so it is with you. We are in charge of our attitudes."

Make Lemonade

Keep in mind that no situation is inherently good or bad. You choose how you're going to feel about that situation.

For example, on the surface it might seem like a total disaster when your horse goes lame, you have an injury that prevents you from riding, or you get eliminated at a show because your horse is behaving so badly. It's understandable that your first reaction might be, "Why me? This is terrible!" But look at it this way. You've been handed a lemon. Go *make lemonade*.

Look at the lemon that was handed to Christopher Reeve. He's made a whole barrel full of lemonade. Most of us would agree that his life-altering riding accident was devastating. Yet, here he is taking that tragedy and turning it around to do triumphant work. He's using his celebrity status to do what he might consider the most important work of his life—making the public away of the importance of research for spinal cord injuries.

So the next time you're faced with a less-than-ideal situation, instead of asking, "Why me," *ask a better question*. Ask, "What's good about this?" "What can I learn from this situation?" or, "How can I use this?" By *asking a better question*, you'll change your focus and begin to see you're in control of what events mean to you. (See pp. 151 and 156, for more about *asking a better question*.)

Let's look at some lemons and figure out how you can *make lemonade*. Your horse is lame or you have an injury. Terrific! Use the extra time to read all those books on riding theory that have been sitting on your shelf. Audit some seminars or clinics given by trainers you admire. Often, you can learn more by sitting and soaking up a day's worth of information than you can during one mounted session on your own horse.

You just got eliminated at your last show because your horse was so fresh he wouldn't listen to you and was very naughty. Great! You now realize that you need to modify your horse show strategy. Plan to get to your next show earlier, even the night before, to allow your horse more time to settle in and adjust to his surroundings. Maybe longe him in the morning to let him blow off a little steam, or take him out for an extra ride early in the day before you actually have to compete.

How about the times when you're frustrated and discouraged because you're struggling to develop a particular skill or teach your horse a new movement and no matter how hard you try, you just can't seem to get it? How can you *make lemonade* out of your frustration? Well, understand that when you experience strong, negative emotions, you're driven to problem-solve. Your frustration forces you to be creative and come up with a solution. Instead of getting frustrated and overwhelmed with training issues, see them as learning opportunities. When you're frustrated, get excited! It means that you're about to have a breakthrough. Get enthusiastic about the skills you're being "forced" to develop. After all, if your

Instead of getting frustrated with training issues, see them as learning opportunities.

horse were perfect all of the time, you'd never have the chance to practice, refine, and improve your riding and training.

CASE HISTORY

Ann

My student, Ann, is a good example of someone who learned to make lemonade. One day in early January, we were having a lesson in preparation for the first big show of the Florida circuit. Since the sessions are private, it's usually easy for the rider to focus on my input and on her horse. On this particular day, however, our little world was uncharacteristically chaotic.

Apparently, some "snowbirds" from the North had decided to take a much needed break from wintry weather and combine their vacation with watching some of the top competitors at the upcoming horse show. Those who had arrived a few days prior to the show were enjoying touring Wellington by stopping in at different barns to watch the training. Several of them were hanging out along the fence line watching Ann's lesson.

Instead of getting angry like this, learn to use a difficult situation to your advantage rather than letting it get the best of you.

In addition, some of the neighbors had brought their horses over to our ring. Not all of these riders knew the "rules of the road," which include passing left hand to left hand as you do when you drive your car and, if you're just walking, staying off the rail. To add to the chaos, there were a couple of loose dogs bounding in and out of the arena enjoying a noisy game of tag.

Ann was quite distracted by all this commotion. She felt the people watching were probably being critical of her horse and her riding. She was annoyed with the other riders in the ring during her private lesson time, and she was irritated with the dogs. From the look on her face, you'd think she had been sucking on one of those lemons! The angrier she got at the situation, the tighter her body became and the worse she rode, and consequently, the worse her horse went. I watched this scene unfold for a while, and then called her over to me.

We discussed the situation, and I asked her what was good about it. Ann's immediate reaction was to snap, "Nothing!" But when she thought about it, she realized that she was being presented with a fabulous opportunity. In fact, we couldn't have designed this scenario better if we had tried.

In one week, she was going to deal with exactly the same distractions she was having to cope with that day. There would be people watching her. There would be other riders in the warm-up area and not all of them would pass left hand to left hand or stay off the rail when walking. There might even be the occasional loose dog or horse to deal with. What a fabulous dress rehearsal for the horse show!

Rather than get upset, she could use the chaos as a golden opportunity to develop her ability to focus and stay in a *cocoon of concentration* despite all the distractions. Not only that, she could also benefit from being able to *practice without the pressure* of having to compete. When Ann realized that she could *make lemonade* by taking advantage of *practicing without pressure*, she totally changed her attitude. She ended up enjoying the challenge of staying focused, had quite a good ride, and was very pleased with her newly discovered concentration skills.

What had changed? Certainly not the commotion in and around the ring. The surroundings were exactly the same. What had changed was Ann's attitude. She made a decision to enjoy the task of staying focused rather than be irritated by the situation. She found satisfaction in being able to block out distractions, and she appreciated the opportunity of having a chance to rehearse and *practice without pressure*.

Choose an Attitude of Gratitude

Probably the best attitude you can choose is an *attitude of gratitude.* When your *winning attitude* falters, ask yourself this question. "What am I grateful for?"

Talk show host Oprah Winfrey thinks this is one of the most important questions we can ask ourselves. She suggests keeping a "gratitude journal" where, each day, you jot down five things that you're grateful for. If you can't think of anything on a particular day, write down that you're breathing!

I love Oprah's idea and started my own gratitude journal. Themes that appear frequently in my journal include: my husband, family, friends, my eyesight, dancing, my dog, beautiful weather, bright colors, horses, the sound of rain on the skylight, chocolate, soft breezes, the smell of the ocean, air conditioning, health, laughter, mountains, music, animals, exercise, my education, good food, puppies, solitude, the smell of flowers, singing, being loved, sunshine, the view from my house, work, days off, dawn, rocking chairs, movies, strong muscles, my ability to teach, books, going to Florida in the winter, and having the freedom to make my own schedule.

Preserving Your Winning Attitude

Maintaining a *winning attitude* isn't easy. After all, we're surrounded by negativity. Just pick up the newspaper or turn on the news and what do you hear? We're deluged with news of terrorism, economic disaster, murders, bombings at high schools, pollution, and scandals. It's not just the media that inundates us with bad news. How about the people you see each day? Some of these *stinkin' thinkers* might even be your family or best friends. It's an interesting phenomenon that when you're around people who complain, pretty soon you're complaining too. That's because *stinkin' thinking* is like a contagious disease. Hang around with complainers long enough, and before you know it, you're infected.[2]

Maybe your typical day begins with you waking up in the morning feeling great. Then you get in the car with members of your carpool and the driver complains about the traffic and how some jerk just cut him off. You get to work, and your co-workers whine about the boss and how the pay is so lousy they can hardly make ends meet. You can't wait until the workday is over so you can head to the barn to ride your horse.

But when you arrive at the barn, you're greeted by your friends who complain about the weather. It's been raining so much and it's so wet outside that they're stuck riding indoors again. It's dreary in the indoor arena and the footing is lousy. As you pick up on their negative vibes, you add that it's particularly bad for you because your horse is so bored with being indoors that he's getting sour and you're sure to have a terrible ride. You started the day enthusiastically, and ended up feeling frustrated and depressed because you were infected with the "negativity" disease.

What if I walked into your home with a great big plastic bag filled with coffee grounds, chicken bones, onion peels, and eggshells, went into your living room and turned the bag dumping all that trash on your living room floor? Do you think you would say to me, "Thank you, Jane, for dumping all your garbage in my house?" I doubt it. I imagine you'd tell me to grab a mop and clean it up.

Well, the garbage that the *stinkin' thinkers* dump into your mind is much more harmful than the garbage I dumped in your house. You're wrong if you think that their words can't hurt you. The truth is that every thought that goes into your mind affects your body chemistry within a split second, and you need to protect and preserve your *winning attitude* at all costs.[3]

Dilute the Negative

It's unrealistic to think you can preserve your attitude by pretending garbage and negativity aren't out there. This stick-your-head-in-the-sand approach really doesn't work.

So what can you do with all the negativity that surrounds you? Take a proactive approach and *dilute the negative*. Read good books. Attend stimulating lectures. Listen to inspiring audiotapes. Watch uplifting movies. Spend your time with positive people. Remember, attitude is contagious. If you want to foster a winning attitude, expose yourself to enthusiastic, positive people.

Make sure to *dilute the negative* on a regular basis. After all, how often do you feed your body? If you're like me, you eat three or four times a day, and if I miss a meal, everyone knows about it. My refrain becomes, "I haven't eaten all day," or, "I haven't eaten since breakfast." It's interesting that we make such a big deal about eating regularly when we tend to only feed our minds occasionally and when it's convenient. After all, from the neck down, we're worth about one hun-

dred dollars, but from the neck up, there's no limit to our worth. So be sure to make time not only to nourish your body but also your mind.

I'm not saying you have to devote several hours each day to reading. Read a couple of paragraphs in the morning before you go out. It sets the tone for your entire day. Or, read for fifteen minutes before you fall asleep at night. The point is to get some positive input on a regular, predetermined schedule.

Make time every day to nourish your mind with positive input.

Debris in the River

One of the most fun images I use to preserve my *winning attitude* is what I call *debris in the river*.

I start by visualizing that I'm standing on a bridge over a river. It's a very polluted river. As I look down at the water, I notice all kinds of debris such as styro-

Say out loud, "Debris in the river," as you picture the unpleasant events of your day floating on by.

foam cups, Big Mac wrappers, and soda cans. I'm totally aware that the river is polluted, but I don't lean over, pick up some of the trash, hug it to my chest, make it mine, and take it home with me. Instead, I watch the garbage slowly flow on by. While I watch, I say out loud, *"Debris in the river."* Then, rather than obsessing about unpleasant things that happened during my day, I say *"Debris in the river,"* as I watch whatever has bothered me flow on by.

This technique also works particularly well when you've had to deal with someone who has upset you. Simply picture that person in the river. Watch her bob along on the surface of the water as you say, *"Debris in the river."* If nothing else, the image will give you a good laugh and you'll end up feeling a lot better.

Dealing with Criticism

As riders, we're surrounded by constant criticism—from ourselves, from our peers, and from the experts. Somehow, we always seem to fall short. We're never quite good enough, talented enough, clever enough, or coordinated enough. In the face of all this negativity, our confidence wavers and our attitude plummets.

Just because we're bombarded by criticism, however, doesn't mean we have to let it affect our attitude. We can deal with criticism in a productive way by arming ourselves with some simple coping strategies.

• Start with perhaps your most unforgiving critic—yourself. Are you crippling yourself with criticism? First, take a moment to really listen to your self-talk. Do you recognize yourself in any of the following statements?

"My right hand seems to have a life of its own; I'm always yanking on the right rein."

"I'm not very good at staying focused when I'm surrounded by distractions."

"I hope no one watches my test because I know it's going to be a disaster."

"What a jerk I was to…(you fill in the blank).

Does this sound like the kind of verbal abuse you inflict on your fragile ego? Why are you beating yourself up because you're not perfect? Keep in mind that perfection is unattainable, and therefore an unrealistic goal. Be a little kinder to yourself by learning to be satisfied with *striving for excellence* rather than perfection. To do the very best you can every single day is a realistic and rewarding goal. Think

At least she hasn't fallen off today!

Think of yourself as a Work In Major Progress (WIMP). Your goal is progress, not perfection.

of yourself as a *WIMP*—a Work In Major Progress! Your goal is progress, not perfection. Every small step forward is a positive sign of growth.

Next, adopt a new motto: *Perceive, don't judge.* Recognize that your seat needs to be more independent, your horse should be "rounder," or that you ought to get fit. Pay attention to the areas that need work and start doing something about them without becoming emotionally involved or overly critical.

And, above all, bear in mind that the greatest conversation you have every day is the one you have with yourself. Be sure to treat yourself with respect. Remember, your subconscious mind hears and believes everything you say, so belittling yourself is totally counterproductive because your put-downs become a *self-fulfilling prophecy.*

Now, consider the criticism that comes from your peers. Don't let "sideline specialists" and "armchair authorities" who've never trained a horse lure you into finding fault with those who are out there putting themselves on the line. It doesn't take a whole lot of talent to pick out what's wrong. On the contrary, it takes some thought and creativity to be able to identify the good qualities and to point out in a constructive way what can be done to improve the whole picture. For example, rather than simply saying, "That horse looks so dull," acknowledge that the horse is relaxed, his rhythm is regular, and with a little more impulsion, he could be quite impressive.

I recall standing on the sidelines with a group of friends watching a Grand Prix test at a Regional Finals. One horse was particularly tense and some of the spectators were shaking their heads while muttering about how terrible the ride was. They went so far as to say that the rider had no business being there. I remarked that considering that the horse was "ballistic," I thought the rider was doing a brilliantly tactful job just keeping him in the ring! Always remember that unless you're the one actually sitting on the animal, it's difficult to know what someone else is struggling with. So, ride a mile in someone else's boots before you criticize their riding.

How about comments from the experts? Do you take it personally when judges and trainers criticize you? Keep in mind that these people are in the business of critiquing your riding and training. It's part of their job. Their observations are not value judgments or reflections on your worth as a human being, and having a bad ride does not make you

a "bad" person. Their comments are merely a mirror of your work at a given moment in time, providing you the information you need to reach a higher standard.

Avoid letting side-line specialists who've never trained a horse lure you into finding fault with others.

That's not to say that you'll never run into a negative trainer or instructor. I remember giving a seminar, and one of the participants told me that the clinician who came to her area on a regular basis was rude and insulting. He belittled the riders and undermined everyone's confidence. She was in a quandary because she felt the knowledge and feedback he gave about the horses was so valuable that she had to subject herself to his abuse and deal with her bruised psyche later. Since you won't ride very well if you're not confident, I personally don't believe that's a fair tradeoff. I suggested that she audit his clinics for the information, and then go to someone else for her own training. If enough riders boycotted these so-called "teachers," they'd have to change their verbally abusive tactics if they wanted to stay in business!

As long as we're taking a good, hard look at keeping criticism in perspective, let's not ignore the fact that the experts rarely seem to agree with each other. I believe that this is the nature of a sport filled with artistic, passionate people. If you ask ten different trainers their opinions on one subject, you're probably going to get ten very different (and strongly stated) opinions. That's not to say that any one person is necessarily right or wrong. Usually it means that individuals prioritize things differently. One professional emphasizes rhythm, another concentrates on relaxation, and a third might focus on impulsion. They're all right, and they generally agree on what the final picture should look like. Each one has merely chosen a slightly different road to Rome!

Dealing with Disappointment

Developing a *winning attitude* might sound great in theory, but what do you do if you've had a huge disappointment? Do you have to put on a happy face all the time? Not necessarily. It's not only okay to grieve for a loss, it's essential. There's no such thing as successfully burying your feelings. Eventually, those feelings come back to haunt you. Instead, recognize the loss. Grieve for it but—and this is a big "but"—put a time limit on it.

That's how I dealt with the disappointment of falling one person short of making the Olympic team for Barcelona. Being on that team had been a huge goal for me for a very long time, and I was crushed when it didn't happen. I decided to let myself really grieve for the loss of that goal. And grieve I did. I drove everyone around me nuts while allowing myself to wallow in despair, but I put a two-week time limit on my grief. When those two weeks were over, time was up. I picked myself up, started looking forward, and went on with my life. I had recognized and acknowledged my disappointment. Then I put it away and soldiered on to the next goal.

If Your Attitude Is Right, the Facts Don't Matter

A *winning attitude* is a very powerful force. So powerful, in fact, that when your attitude is right, the "facts" don't matter. The "facts" are all the logical reasons why it would be impossible for you to reach your goal. Understanding that *attitude* is more important than *facts* was a huge "lightbulb moment" for me.

For as long as I can remember, I had dreamed of being an elite athlete. As a little girl, I watched the Olympics on television and became mesmerized by the athletes. It didn't matter what sport it was or what country the athletes were from; I was moved to tears by their struggles and victories.

List 1:
You won't make it because:
no horse
no equipment
no money
no time
you are a klutz

List 2:
You can make it because you:
have the right attitude
have a fire in the belly
are committed to a goal
believe in yourself
are determined to improve

Attitude is more important than facts.

As I've mentioned already, when I was in my twenties, my dream took the form of becoming a member of the USET and representing my country in international competition. I couldn't imagine anything more exciting than earning the privilege of wearing my country's flag when I cantered down the centerline. Now that I've done that, it sounds like it was a perfectly reasonable goal. But, at

Here I am, age 9, on Lady Kansas.

the time, I was light years away from being able to reach it. I had a long list of "facts" that were stacked against me. Logically, those "facts" should have made it nearly impossible for me to succeed.

First and foremost, I didn't have a horse. The second fact was that I didn't have any money to buy a horse. At the time, I was waitressing for most of the year and taught riding in a summer camp six days a week for the staggering amount of seventy-five dollars! When I finally purchased a broken-down Thoroughbred off the track, he cost me my entire savings: five hundred dollars. As you can imagine, he was hardly an international prospect.

My list of facts went on and on. When I made my goal, I had only ridden through First Level. First Level was a long way from Grand Prix. Physically, I was hardly the picture of an elite athlete. I was a good twenty pounds overweight and smoked three packs of cigarettes a day. To add to my physical challenges, although I was athletic, I was not innately gifted. I was one of those riders who had to plug along and, in a very mechanical way, learn to ride.

When I started to show, I realized that I was a very nervous competitor. I was so anxious that I could barely sleep the night before a show. Eating during the competition was out of the question, and I spent more than my fair share of time in the "Porta-John." Also, by nature, I wasn't much of a risk taker. I was afraid to go out on a limb because I might fail. You know the scenario: Stay in your *comfort zone* so you don't get hurt.

Fire in Your Belly

That list of facts should have been enough to discourage me from going after my dream, but my attitude was right, and I had another big plus going for me. I had a burning desire—a *fire in my belly*—to reach my goal. You need that kind of passion because you're always going to encounter obstacles and setbacks. If you don't want to reach your goal so badly that you can taste it, those obstacles are going to stop you right in your path.

Wanting something so badly that you have *fire in your belly* gives you the resolve and commitment to pay the price. The biggest price I had to pay was to quit smoking and get fit. I felt so passionately about becoming an elite athlete that I was willing to make those changes.

CASE HISTORY

Alice

You really are unstoppable when you have *fire in your belly*. That point is brilliantly illustrated in a letter I received from a woman who wrote to me about her personal challenges. In her letter she explained:

"I have been riding since childhood but acquired a Traumatic Brain Injury (TBI) in October, 1992. It was classified as severe. I could not even control my body or speak. Eventually, I learned to talk again, although my speech is still slow. The doctors say I won't improve.

"But I don't listen to doctors' predictions anymore. If I did, I wouldn't be doing what I am. For instance, I saw a neurologist about six months after the initial trauma, and she said I wouldn't improve any further. At first I cried, thinking she must know. Then I decided to prove her wrong.

"I had ridden for most of my life, and was just crushed when I tried to ride and couldn't even mount. I didn't give up though. I tried again at a stable that served disabled riders. Through that experience, I gained confidence, and about a year and a half after starting there, I began learning from a regular trainer.

"I now own a horse who meets my goals as a teammate. He has both the physical and emotional talents to eventually compete at international levels."

This woman had a passion to ride again. That *fire in her belly* gave her the resolve to live her dream when she could have just as easily used her disability as a good excuse to remain an invalid.

Leave Excuses Behind

Sometimes, when we look at all the facts that are stacked against us, we get overwhelmed. As a result, we come up with all sorts of excuses why we don't commit ourselves to our goals.

The list of excuses we invent can cover a lot of territory. Perhaps you've heard yourself say, "I'm too old, too young, too fat, too thin, too busy, too broke, too inexperienced, too crippled, not the right type, not talented enough, don't have enough time, lack credibility, am overwhelmed by demands, am burned out, insecure, or too impatient to qualify for the finals, compete at a higher level, start a business, change career, or get fit."

It's perfectly normal to come up with excuses like these. In fact, we need those solid, inarguable reasons to justify abandoning our dreams and goals because we're *not* crazy. If I had said to my friends, "Gee, I'd love to be a member of the equestrian team, but I don't have a top horse, and I don't have the money to get one," my friends would commiserate with me. They'd say, "We know. We'd love to do that too. But it's impossible because you just don't have the financial resources to pursue that goal." My excuses and my friends' confirmation of those excuses would give me permission to stay in my *comfort zone*. It's very comfortable in the *comfort zone*, but as I said earlier, it's also boring and not very challenging. It's much more interesting to step out of the *comfort zone* into the *achievement zone*.

One of my clinic participants wrote to tell me how she moved herself into the *achievement zone*. She could have easily used her crippled knees as an excuse to give up her riding goals. Instead, she modified her program to suit her disability. She explained:

"Because of arthritis in both of my knees (too many years of professional tennis plus I had my third, double-knee surgery in February) I had felt that I couldn't reach my goals in dressage...I decided to re-evaluate my goals and "just do it"! Thank goodness the new rules make posting optional—that is a BIG no for me, per my doctor. I love dressage! And if I can't post, so what! I'll do what I can and have fun with it. I'm not out to compete at the Olympics. I'm doing this for the sheer joy of dancing with my partner."

She went on to tell me that she started incorporating *visualization* into her riding. She decided, however, not to tell her trainer what she was doing. She wanted to see if her trainer could see a difference. Obviously, she did: During one training session her trainer's comment was, "I wish I had taped today's session. Your seat has improved soooooo much! What are you doing differently?"

You, too, can move yourself out of your *comfort zone* into your *achievement zone.* Start by leaving your excuses behind.

You can do this symbolically by making an *excuse box.* Put the box in your tack room. Write your excuses on a piece of paper and drop the paper in the box before you get on your horse. If you find that you're so attached to your excuses that you can't bear to leave them behind, take them out of the box when you finish riding. Just be sure to make your "deposit" again the next day before you put your foot in the stirrup.

After hearing about my excuse box, one seminar participant told me about her "'I can' can." She said that each time her children said, "I can't do this or that," she had them write, "I can _____ ." Then they had to put the piece of paper in the "'I can' can." I thought this was a great idea. After all, if you think you can or you can't, you're right!

Write down your excuses and leave them behind before you get on your horse.

Essentials of Attitude

- Success is eighty-five percent attitude, fifteen percent technical skill.
- When life hands you lemons, *make lemonade.*
- Attitude is a choice. It's up to you to choose how you're going to react to the hand you're dealt.
- Preserve your *winning attitude* by:

    1. Avoiding *stinkin' thinkers.*

    2. *Diluting the negative* regularly by reading good books, attending stimulating lectures, listening to inspiring audiotapes, and watching uplifting movies.

    3. Learning to cope with criticism from yourself, your peers, and the experts.

    4. Learning to deal with disappointment.

- Be a *W.I.M.P.*—a Work In Major Progress. Your goal is *progress not perfection.*
- If your attitude is right, the facts don't matter.
- Develop an *attitude of gratitude.*
- If you have a *fire in your belly,* you'll be able to stay on track when the going gets rough.
- Dare to step out of your *comfort zone* into the *achievement zone.*
- Make an *excuse box* and leave your excuses behind.

W e all have days when we feel a little down or crabby, but it's important to be even-tempered in order for training to run smoothly. If you're up one day and down the next, you're going to frustrate and confuse your horse.

It's important to control your moods because your horse needs you to be consistent—consistent in your expectation of him, consistent in the way you ask him to do things, and consistent with reward. If you're inconsistent because you're on an emotional roller coaster, he's not going to understand what you want.

One thing you can do to level out your moods is to stop taking yourself too seriously. Adopt the *cosmic perspective.* People with the *cosmic perspective*

If you are inconsistent because you are on an emotional roller coaster, you will confuse and upset your horse.

don't sweat the small stuff. They realize how unimportant most things are in the big picture and they learn to enjoy each moment. They look for fun in every situation and even delight in having a laugh at their own expense.

Why is it so important to enjoy yourself and have fun in all kinds of situations? In the first place, you're doing yourself a favor because having fun contributes to the kind of *winning attitude* you need for peak performance. Secondly, having fun creates the right physiology within your body. Research has shown that

Michael Kohl
on Visette;
with his nephew,
Mikey

when you laugh, blood pressure and heart rate go way up at first, but both go way down afterward. Heart rate can even drop fifteen beats below resting rate. Plus, laughing causes a huge endorphin release that contributes to an overall feeling of well-being.

So, make a point of finding ways to have fun. Go to shows with friends who get raucous and make you laugh. The less intense you are and the more fun you have, the better. When you hear the announcer call your equitation class into the ring, say under your breath, "Oh, yippee! It's my turn!" Go around the ring and as you pass the judge, pretend you're going to give him a wink. Think, do, and say whatever silly thing it takes for you to have fun.

I remember how much we enjoyed sharing a laugh with one of our friends, Michael Kohl, at one of the big dressage shows in Wellington, Florida. It was a very windy morning when Michael entered the arena for his Prix St. Georges test on the first day of competition. During the first movement, which was an extended trot across the diagonal, the combination of a lot of wind and the surge of the extension blew his very expensive silk top hat right off his head. As it happened, the hat landed in the middle of the arena in the very path that Michael was going to have to take several times during the course of his test. Since Michael refused to stomp on his hat, much of his test looked as if it was ridden by a drunken sailor! Needless to say, his score reflected his wobbly ride.

The second day of the show was just as windy as the first. However, Michael came up with a very creative solution to his top hat woes. In order to keep his hat from blowing off, he weather-stripped it to his head! This would have been a brilliant idea except that Michael forgot one thing. Men normally remove their top hats at the beginning and end of their tests to salute the judge. Michael cantered down the centerline and came to a precise, perfectly square halt. He tried to remove his top hat for the salute but realized that his hat was so securely in place that the only way he was going to be able to remove it was to drop the reins and use both hands. He tugged and pulled on that hat until it finally came off like a suction cup reluctantly releasing its grip.

At this point, you might think that all was well. However, even though Michael was able to remove his hat, the weather stripping remained securely in place around his head! He slowly peeled it off, rolled it into a ball, dropped it at his horse's feet, picked up the reins and continued with the test as if nothing out of the ordinary had happened.

All of us, including Michael, had a hearty laugh over his top hat adventure. Whenever the atmosphere became a bit too intense throughout the rest of the show, all we had to do to lighten the mood was think about his escapade.

Moody to Even-Tempered

TIPS FOR CHANGE

- Conquer moodiness by adopting the *cosmic perspective*. It will insure that you don't sweat the small stuff.
- Lighten your mood by *having a good laugh.* Laughing creates the right physiology within your body.
- Think, do, and say whatever silly thing helps you have fun.

17

Punch Up Self-Talk and Speech

Censor Yourself

B efore you can use self-talk to help you achieve your goals, you need to become aware of the words that come out of your mouth. In many cases, you sabotage yourself by your choice of words without even realizing it.

For example, a woman came up to me at one of the big shows in Florida. She was very enthusiastic and excited and started to tell me about herself, but as she spoke, the "caution lights" in my head started going off. On the surface, she sounded very positive, destined to make her dream a reality. Unfortunately, the words she used to tell me about herself were the very words that would make it difficult, if not impossible, to reach her goals. Here's what she said:

"I want to make it to the top with my riding and I know I can do it. I always try to do my very best. My horse is really talented even though he's difficult at times, especially the first day of a show. I have to admit that sometimes he's so fresh that I'm afraid of getting hurt. I hate it when I feel like that. It's been a real long-term problem for me, but my first goal is not to obsess about it.

"Plus, I'm really serious, but I'm broke and can't swing going to Florida in the winter to train full-time like everyone else does. If I had consistent help, I know I could do it!"

On the surface, this sounds like a fairly ordinary and benign conversation. In fact, you've probably had discussions like it hundreds of times without realizing just how much damage you were doing. The words that set off my caution lights were: "try," "difficult," "afraid," "hate," "problem," "not," "broke," "can't," and "if." Wow! That's a lot of negative self-talk and damaging software for her to install into her mental computer.

The truth is that she could have that same conversation with me without sabotaging herself in the process. To do this, she first needs to become more aware of her self-talk. Then, she needs to either completely eliminate certain words, or substitute other words that would help, rather than hinder, her efforts.

Let's go through the words one at a time, starting with "try." "Try" is one of those words that you should simply eliminate from your vocabulary when you're talking about your goals. The word "try" carries a built-in excuse. When you "try" to do your best, you're basically admitting that you're not committed to achieving your goal.

The fact is, you can always do your best. Maybe, at this moment in time your best isn't world-class, but you can certainly ride to the best of your current ability. Then, as you develop your skills, you raise the bar and your best becomes better. Your commitment to doing your best remains constant while the standard of your riding changes as you learn and grow.

Here's an exercise that illustrates the problem with the word "try." Close your eyes and think about riding to a four-foot jump. "Try" to jump it. Now open your eyes, take a deep breath, and close your eyes again. This time ride to the jump and soar over it.

How did you see yourself and your horse when you "tried" to jump the fence? Did you see your horse struggling? Hesitating? Refusing? Running Out? Knocking down the top rail? Were you nervous and full of doubt about whether you'd make it over without a crash or a knockdown?

How did you see yourself when you pictured cantering to the fence and soaring over it? Did you see yourself clearing it with inches to spare? Did it feel effortless and exhilarating? Were you calm and confident?

Think about it. When you "tried" to jump, you saw yourself expending effort. Maybe you were successful and maybe you weren't, but the attempt was full of effort, and you weren't totally committed to successfully clearing the fence. However, when you saw yourself soaring over the fence, you did it easily and with conviction.

The point is that the word "try," has the connotation that you're going to put a lot of effort into something without necessarily succeeding. So, don't "try" to do something. Commit yourself to doing it!

The next phrase that hit me was, "he's difficult." By saying that, she's guaranteed to be in for a struggle. Her words become a self-fulfilling prophecy. To be her own best friend rather than her own worst enemy, she needs to reword that statement. She can say something like, "He used to be really difficult at shows, but he's getting much better. So much better in fact, that by the second day of the show, he's like he is at home. I'm sure that with more mileage, eventually he'll be as relaxed the first day as he is on the second day."

The word "try" is counterproductive. Don't "try" to succeed...

After that she says, "I'm afraid of getting hurt." Bingo! She's just given her subconscious mind another negative target. Instead, she should say something like, "I used to be afraid of getting hurt, but I know I'm very capable and well-prepared. I can pretty much handle anything that comes my way."

The next word she needs to eliminate from her vocabulary is "hate." As soon as you say you hate something, such as, "I hate the footing," "I hate riding when it's windy," "This judge hates

...succeed!

my horse," you make it impossible to do well. Barbra Schulte, author of the audiotape series, *Mentally Tough Riding*, explains that when you make strong negative statements like this, you create a corresponding body chemistry that limits you physically. Turn the negative around by saying, "love" instead of "hate." Instead of saying that she hates feeling afraid of getting hurt, this woman can say, "I love the challenge!" You can say "I love the footing," "I love riding when it's windy," "This judge loves my horse!" If nothing else, you'll have a good chuckle over what you just said. As I said in *Moodiness*, laughing always relieves tension and promotes well-being.

Challenge yourself by *asking a better question*, "How can I cleverly warm up on this footing so I can get the best performance from my horse?" Or, "How can I keep my horse so mentally involved in the training process that he's not distracted by the wind?" Or, "How can we have such a harmonious ride that we change this judge's mind about my horse?" (See page 156 for more.)

The next word that set off my internal alarm was "problem." When you say things are a problem, you set yourself up to feel overwhelmed. How about substituting the word "challenge?" Or better yet, how about "opportunity?" I like "opportunity" because it gives me a built-in feeling of being able to overcome any obstacle. For example, instead of saying she has a "long-term" problem, she might say that her horse's behavior gives her the opportunity to practice some of her relaxation exercises so she can better cope with his antics.

She then says, "...my first goal is not to obsess about it." Remember, there is no picture in the mind for the word "not." Therefore, her mind skips right over the word "not." Its target becomes "...my first goal is to obsess about it." It would be much better for her to say that her first goal is to let her fears float right on by like *debris in the river.*

She goes on to say she's "broke." She's just given herself another terrible target! How about, "I may not have the money right now, but I'm very resourceful and I'll find a way. Maybe, I'll be a working student for the winter, or hire myself out to do some braiding at shows this summer to earn some extra cash. Maybe, I'll apply for a scholarship from our local riding club."

Then she says she "can't swing going to Florida." "Can't" is another word like "try" and "hate." She needs to eliminate it from her vocabulary. Remember, if you think you can or you think you can't, you're right! The other thing she can do is replace, "I can't," with "I must." Her self-talk becomes, "I *must* swing going to Florida." This is good advice for any of your "can'ts." Change your mantra to, "If I can't, then I must." For example, "If I can't sit the trot, then I must sit the trot." "If I can't relax, then I must relax."

Speaking of the word "must," think about the message you send your subconscious when you say you "should" ride more regularly, compared to saying you "must" ride more regularly. Keep in mind that we don't always get our "shoulds," but we always get our "musts."[1]

Last but not least, she says, "If I had the help..." She needs to change that "if" to "when." Her statement becomes, "When I have consistent help, I know I can do it!" In this way, she's telling her subconscious that she's sure it's going to happen.

See how easy it is to sabotage yourself with a seemingly innocent conversation? It's also just as easy to censor your speech and have the same conversation without inadvertently undermining your efforts. Just develop an ear for the negative words that come out of your mouth, then eliminate those words or substitute positive ones instead.

Self-Fulfilling Prophecy

In Chapter 7, I explained how visualization enhances training on two levels. On one level, your own body responds to the picture in your mind's eye. On another level, your horse "reads" the picture in your mind and reacts to it as well.

I believe the same two-fold effect exists with self-talk. When you repeatedly say that your horse is a pig or a brat, your language affects your attitude toward him. You'll most likely treat him less kindly and patiently than if you say that he is honest, generous, and eager-to-please.

Your language also affects your horse. Whatever you say about him tends to become a *self-fulfilling prophecy*. He'll act in a way that supports your impression. So what would you like him to be—a brat or a gentleman? The choice is yours.

I always tell every horse I ride that he is the BEST horse I know. I tell him over and over again that he is wonderful, perfect, and brilliant. I just make sure that when I do this, the other horses I ride aren't within earshot because each one thinks that he's my favorite!

Ease your way into using these new techniques.

Where Do I Start?

Sometimes, when we look at ourselves objectively, it seems as if there's so much to do that it's hard to know where to begin. We can get so overwhelmed that we don't even start making changes. One of the simplest ways to start is with *affirmations*, which I introduced to you in Chapter 11, page 97.

I suggest easing your way into using *affirmations* in the same way that you eased your way into visualization. Start small and focus on just a part of your body or your

horse's body. For example, you might decide to focus on your hands. Your self-talk could be, "My hands are soft and quiet." Or, you might decide to focus on your horse's hind legs. In that case, your self-talk could be, "My horse's hind legs are active and energetic."

You can also ease your way into changing your attitude and skill level. Begin by pinpointing the areas where you need the most help. Take the following quiz to determine how to prioritize what you need to work on first, and allot the appropriate number to each statement:

1 strongly disagree
2 disagree somewhat
3 neither agree nor disagree strongly
4 agree somewhat
5 agree strongly

Quiz
I am always patient with my horse.
I am even-tempered.
I give aids clearly and consistently.
I reward my horse often.
I am confident and relaxed when I ride at home.
I am confident and relaxed out on the trail.
I am confident and relaxed when I compete.
I am confident and relaxed when I take my horse to new places.
I am confident and relaxed when I try new exercises.
I am confident and relaxed when I jump.
I am bold when I ride.
I am calm in new situations.
I am a receptive student.
I am well prepared before I go to a show.
I am easy to coach at a show.
I am focused at home.
I am focused at shows.
I always remember my test/course/pattern.

I am optimistic about my riding.

I am flexible in my training.

I bounce back quickly from disappointment.

I love a challenge.

I am very disciplined.

I am proactive rather than passive when I ride.

I am committed to my goals.

I am very motivated to improve my riding.

I am physically fit.

I am a good problem-solver.

I am open to change.

I am willing to take risks.

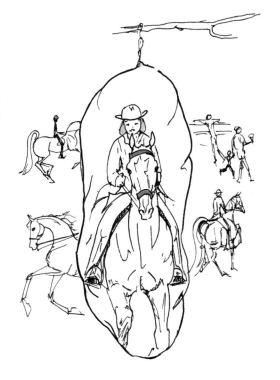

Look back over the quiz. Which statements have the lowest numbers? Maybe five statements scored a one or a two. That's your starting point. Pick two of those five statements depending on what you want to change the most. Your homework is to spend just four minutes a day working on each of these issues. No matter how busy you are, I know you can find four minutes a day to make some positive changes in your riding.

As an example, we'll say that two of your lowest scores reveal that you're not very focused at shows and you often lose your temper when you ride.

Spend one of your four minutes visualizing yourself in total concentration at a show. There are lots of horses in the warm-up area whizzing every which way. Spectators are milling about. Yet, even with all this activity, you remain totally focused. You and your horse are enveloped in your *cocoon of concentration.* Nothing exists outside that cocoon. For the next minute, repeat out loud, "I am totally focused at competitions. I am totally focused at competitions."

At a busy show, picture yourself inside your *cocoon of concentration.*

Now, on to your next challenge: impatience. For the first minute, visualize yourself remaining patient and calm while doing an exercise with your horse. See him tossing his head, breaking into canter when you want him to trot, pulling on your hands, or shying at the same spot in the ring each time you go by. Regardless of what he does, you remain endlessly patient. You calmly make corrections and remain emotionally detached from his antics. For the next minute, repeat many times, "I have infinite patience. I have infinite patience."

Develop infinite patience by staying emotionally detached from your horse's antics.

Practice the images and self-talk for three weeks, and then take the quiz again. You might be surprised that focus and patience are no longer your biggest challenges. If they are, continue with the same exercises for another three weeks. If not, move on to your next challenge. Look for the next two low score statements. Start visualizing and self-talking your way to success, four minutes at a time.

Ask a Better Question

Another thing to think about is the kind of questions your self-talk asks yourself. Whenever you ask a question, your brain searches for an answer. If you ask a lousy question, all you can get is a lousy answer. "Why" questions are the worst kind because when you ask "why," your brain will always give you an answer to support why things are going wrong.

For example, if you ask yourself "why" you always hang on your horse's mouth instead of keeping your hands softly forward, your brain says, "You pull on the reins because you're stupid and uncoordinated!" If you ask yourself "why" you always space out at shows, your brain answers you by saying, "You space out because you're an idiot." If you ask yourself "why" you're so afraid all the time, your brain answers, "You're afraid because you're a gutless chicken."

So, if you find yourself becoming depressed, discouraged, or frustrated with your riding, chances are you're asking lousy questions. If you want a better answer, you need to *ask a better question.*

The following are some examples of how you can turn a lousy question into a better one.

Why do I always screw up at shows?	*What kind of plan can I come up with to create better results in the ring?*
Why does this always happen to me?	*How can I use this to my advantage?*
Why am I so uncoordinated when I give the aids for lateral work?	*What exercises do I need to practice to become more coordinated?*
Why am I always so broke I can't do what I want with my horse?	*How can I raise more money?*
Why do I get so tense when I ride in front of people?	*What relaxation exercises do I need to learn?*
Why can't I do this?	*How can I do this?*
Why am I so afraid?	*How can I become more calm and confident?*

More Essentials of Self-Talk and Speech

- Start listening to your *self-talk* so you don't sabotage yourself.
- Eliminate "try," "can't," and "hate," from your vocabulary.
- See "problems" as opportunities.
- Let your new mantra be, "If I can't, then I must."
- Turn your "shoulds" into "musts."
- Your self-talk becomes a *self-fulfilling prophecy*.
- Use language that helps you to be positive and proactive.
- Spend four minutes a days working on *changing your software*. Use half of that time visualizing what you want, and the other half, repeating *positive affirmations*.
- If you want a better answer, you need to *ask a better question*.
- Avoid "why" questions.

18

Discouragement

At one time or another, you're going to get discouraged about your riding. This might happen when you think you're just not making any progress. You feel like you're taking two steps forward and three steps back. Maybe it happens when either you or your horse are sidelined with an injury. Perhaps you get discouraged because your horse is so good at home, but he's inattentive or disobedient when away.

Your reactions are perfectly normal, and it's fine to be discouraged for the moment. The problem only exists if you stay that way. The antidote to "getting stuck there" is to be resilient.

Resilience is an important quality in every area of life but it seems particularly necessary if you're going to survive in the horse business. How many times have you been chugging along, smoothly working toward a goal, and then you show up at the barn and discover your horse is lame and needs a month off? How many times have you been in the top placing at a horse trial only to have a rail down in stadium and get knocked out of the ribbons? How many times have you felt like quitting because you're riding so badly? At times like these, your resilience—your bounce-back ability—will help you stay optimistic and ready to soldier on.

It really doesn't matter what the challenge is. You can get knocked down in any area of your life as you pursue your goals. But getting knocked down doesn't matter. You never truly fail unless you quit. And if you're resilient, you'll be able to bounce back after disappointment and stay in the game.

Denny Emerson agrees that resilience is an extremely important quality for riders. I discovered this when we both attended the 2000 American Riding Instructors Association annual meeting in Florida. In a speech to a group of instructors, Denny surprised me by saying that his new hero was Richard Simmons. I, personally, love Richard Simmons, but I couldn't imagine how Denny, a "man's man" who remains fit and trim even as he celebrates his sixty-third birthday, could relate to this flamboyant TV fitness guru.

It became clear to me when Denny explained that Simmons was his new hero because, "Richard never, never gives up on people. He won't give up on you even when you've given up on yourself. He always says, 'Yes, you *can* do it.' And, he knows that you can. It's just figuring out how to push the button that gets you to believe in yourself and stick with it." His bottom line is that if you hang in there, eventually you will prevail.

What gives some people that ability to bounce back after a huge disappointment while others quit and run home with their tail between their legs? Denny thinks it boils down to several factors that add up to this quality we call resilience. It all starts with having a *fire in your belly*. He explained:

"First, you have to be filled with a burning desire. You absolutely have to want to reach your goals so badly that you will do any task, make any change, work twice as hard as the next guy, and even suffer physical discomfort to succeed.

"Secondly, you have to have an unshakable belief in yourself. Look at Kerry Milliken, a highly successful three-day event rider who competed for the U.S. She had H.M.S. Dash and The Pirate and she was on the top of the world. Then she disappeared for ten years. But, eventually she came back with Out and About. It

Kerry Milliken on Out and About at the Burghley Horse Trials, in England, 1997; and winning the three-day event individual bronze medal at the Olympic Games in Atlanta, 1996

was ten long years between those horses, but Kerry never quit thinking that she was a great rider.

"Winners like Kerry see themselves as successful. Disappointments are just temporary setbacks. Setbacks don't defeat them. As a matter of fact, setbacks often motivate them because they annoy them or even make them angry."

Making a decision and committing yourself to your goal and boldness are other factors in resilience. Denny added:

"Until there is decision, there is always hesitancy—the chance to draw back. The moment that one commits, however, all sorts of unforeseen things come along to support your decision. Things that you never would have dreamed of start to happen."

"I have earned a deep respect for one of Goethe's couplets, 'Whatever you can do or dream you can, begin it. Boldness has genius, power and magic in it.' "A lot of the people who keep coming back for more are very bold. I don't mean bold in the sense of the word that they would drive a race car, but bold in the sense that they're going to get what they want. They're going to do whatever it takes to succeed and when they get knocked down, well, that's just a step back.

"Boldness enables you to be resilient because you dare to take a risk and perhaps fail. But, you see, resilient people don't equate failing with *being* a failure. Failing is just a screw-up in the road. It's a temporary aberration from your goal.

"In fact, failing can be a *positive* glitch because it gives you necessary feedback. When something doesn't work for me, I don't think of it as ultimate failure. I think, 'I've screwed up and I'd better not do that again. I'd better go take some lessons and learn how to do this or that.' I think of it merely as a temporary obstacle and I just keep on plugging.

"Last but not least, I also think anger is part of resilience. Anger can be a neg-

Resilient people don't equate failing with being a failure.

ative but very powerful motivator. A lot of people misunderstand the power of anger. If I told you in a negative fashion, 'Give it up little girl. You're not good enough,' your anger might just motivate you. Rather than becoming overwhelmed by despair, you might get really angry and want revenge. 'Damn it! I'll show you. I am NOT going to NOT get this done.'

"I tell the kids I teach that they have to be persistent. I say, 'If you try, if you study and plug, I cannot guarantee in any way that you'll succeed. But I can tell you this for sure. If you don't, I can guarantee that you won't.'"

Discouragement to Resilience

TIPS FOR CHANGE

- It's normal to get discouraged from time to time. It only becomes a problem if you stay there emotionally.
- Resilience allows you to bounce back from being discouraged.
- If you're resilient, obstacles and setbacks won't stop you in your tracks.
- Look at "failure" in a positive light. It gives you necessary feedback. It tells you what doesn't work so you can figure out what does.
- You never really fail unless you quit.
- The factors that make up resilience are:

    Having a *fire in your belly.*
    Believing in yourself.
    Committing yourself to your goal.
    Being bold enough to dare to keep on "keeping on."
    Using hurt, such as anger, as a motivator.

19

Variations to Visualization

Visualization should be fun and, with practice, relatively simple. If you're having trouble, however, there are all sorts of different ways you can make visualizing easier and more enjoyable. In this chapter, I'll look at several variations to visualization:

Use your zoom lens.

Borrow a professional's body or his horse.

Be the director—vary camera angles.

Slow motion.

"Anesthesia" for pain.

Kinesthetic and auditory imagery.

Coping rehearsal.

Create a perfect practice tape.

End-goal imaging and process imaging.

Use Your Zoom Lens

When you first begin using visualization to improve performance, you might feel overwhelmed if you try to picture everything at once. You can ease yourself into the process by using your *zoom lens*.

Using a *zoom lens* is one of my favorite techniques. I choose a specific relevant body part and focus on it. Sometimes, I zoom in on a part of my horse's body, and other times, on a part of mine.

Pick one small aspect of your riding that you'd like to improve. Perhaps you struggle with your balance during transitions from walk to trot. Usually, as your horse surges forward into the trot, you get left behind his movement, your legs fly forward, and you pull on the reins to keep your balance. In your *mind's eye movie*, zoom in on your seat. Watch yourself sitting in perfect balance as your horse moves from walk to trot. Your seat feels like it's glued to the saddle. You hear the squeak of the saddle as your horse steps forward into the trot.

Improve your seat in transitions by imagining wrapping your legs around a barrel and knotting them underneath.

Replay this picture hundreds of time. Take advantage of the time you have when you're not actually riding. This is often the best time to visualize because there are fewer distractions. When you're cooking dinner, driving to work, or drying your hair, do your *perfect practice* over and over again. It might take a couple of weeks for you to feel some changes in your seat, but once you do, you're ready to go on to the next step.

Next, focus on your legs. Feel your legs fastened to your horse's sides as if with Velcro. Imagine that you're sitting on a fifty-five-gallon drum and your legs curve around it like a bow-legged cowboy's. They've become so long that you can knot your ankles underneath your horse's barrel.

Once you have better control over your legs, switch your focus to your hands. As you zoom in on your hands, see how they remain independent of the movement of your horse. They are so still that you could be holding two glasses of water and not spill a drop as your horse moves from the walk to the trot.

Switch your focus to your hands. Picture holding two glasses of water and not spilling a drop.

Recently, I used the *zoom lens* technique to help my mare Konetta. Konetta had been struggling to maintain the activity of her canter during pirouettes. In my mind's eye, I zoomed in on her hind legs. I held a picture of her inside hind leg bending and arcing under her body during each stride of the pirouette. It was easy for me to hold this picture of beautifully engaged hind legs in my mind because I had just returned from watching Arlene "Tuny" Page's magnificent mare, Claire, doing incredible pirouettes in a training session with Conrad Schumacher, coach of the British dressage team at the Olympics in Sydney. While sitting on Konetta, I held the picture of Claire's hind legs firmly in my mind's eye, and Konetta's pirouettes improved dramatically.

I also zoomed in on my seat. The seat determines the tempo or speed of the canter, and with each canter bound, I pictured moving my seat quickly from the back of the saddle toward the front of the saddle. I mimicked the motion that I'd use if I were sitting on a swing and I wanted to swing higher.

Once you are adept at zooming in on and visualizing one aspect of your riding, broaden your focus by practicing a series of movements—an entire dressage test, a reining pattern, or a course of jumps. Even though you're picturing more than one aspect of your riding, keep the level of detail the same as it was when you were zooming in on one thing.

No matter how experienced you become at visualizing the whole picture, you can always return to using your *zoom lens* to narrow your focus back to a single detail. In this way, you can break your mental pictures down into digestible parts. For example, if you're working at keeping your horse on the bit, zoom in on his

Arlene Page is on Claire doing a pirouette

Regulate the tempo of the canter by pushing with your seat as if you wanted to swing higher.

mouth. See the foam on his lips as you visualize him softly chewing on the bit. If your horse tends to be stiff in his poll, imagine he's flexing his poll so that he appears to be looking into a bucket of grain. If his back tends to be stiff, imagine you see it undulating like a trampoline.

Borrow a Professional's Body or His Horse

Another way you can play with visualization is by watching a very accomplished rider, either for real or on videotape, and then *borrow his body or his horse*.

Christine Traurig and Etienne

Let's say you're still struggling with seeing yourself doing transitions from walk to trot. Find some video footage of a beautiful horse and rider, like Christine Traurig and Etienne, members of the bronze-medal-winning Olympic dressage team in Sydney, 2000. Review the tape often enough so that you can clearly hold a picture of them doing transitions from walk to trot in your mind's eye.

Don't work too hard at this. Your subconscious mind takes in the information whether you're concentrating intensely or not. Just let the image of Christine and Etienne passively wash over you again and again. Trust that whatever you've stored in your mental computer will be there when you call on it while riding. When you can see the picture clearly in your imagination, borrow Christine's head and put it on your body much as you'd put on a helmet. Wear her head while you ride your horse.[1]

If you find your horse hard to sit on, you can borrow Etienne as well. While riding your own horse, hold a picture of Etienne in your mind's eye. "Watch" how he stays absolutely steady in his head and neck as he steps into the trot. "Feel" the springiness of his trot as it sucks your seat in and then takes it forward as if you're glued to the saddle.

You're the Director

There are lots of variations to mental rehearsal. Since *you're the director*, you can create your *mind's eye movie* any way you like. For example, you can watch the show as if you're at the movies or you can be the "star of the show." When you watch yourself as if you're at the movies, you're an observer. You can see yourself as a judge or your instructor might. This is called visualizing in a *dissociated* state.

When you're the "star of the show," picture yourself looking out through your own eyes. This is called visualizing in an *associated* state and is actually the more powerful way to visualize.

Start with visualizing in a dissociated state, and when, as an observer, you've seen what you need to do, step into the picture so that you're completely involved in the images.[2]

As the *director of your mind's eye movies*, you can also play with visualization by varying camera angles. Move your camera forty-five degrees to the left or right. Try an overhead camera. Or, watch your ride from the front or from the back. And, as you'll see in the next section, you can even run your movies in slow motion.

Imaging is less powerful when you are sitting and watching from the audience than it is when you are actually in the movie yourself.

Slow Motion

I know from experience that it's unsettling when your ride feels as if it's in fast forward, and you're on to the next movement or jump before you have a chance to make any adjustments or corrections. When too much is happening, too fast, I like to run my *mind's eye movie* in *slow motion*. Practicing in *slow motion* reduces my anxiety because I feel like I have all the time in the world to make corrections and adjustments.

It's easy to learn how to visualize in *slow motion*. Watch some videos of yourself or someone else riding a very good course of jumps, a reining pattern, or a dressage test. Then watch the tape several times in *slow motion*. Once you get a sense of how the ride looks when time passes in *slow motion*, you can recreate it in your imagination.

Anesthesia

Like most athletes, I frequently have to deal with annoying aches and pains. My issues aren't serious but when they occur, they definitely distract me. When I have to deal with pain, I often use visualization to help me. I incorporate a phenomenon called *anesthesia* into my *mind's eye movies*. I learned this from Dr. Janet Edgette, coauthor of *The Handbook of Hypnotic Phenomena in Psychotherapy* and author of *Heads up: Practical Sports Psychology for Riders, Their Trainers, and Their Families.*

Before I go into further detail on how to use visualization to *anesthetize* pain, I want to clarify that you must not use this technique to ignore *acute* pain, which should always receive medical treatment. If your doctor, however, gives you the go-ahead to ride with a chronic problem, or you've been training hard and are having insignificant but annoying muscle pain, you can use this tool to help you deal it.

As with all your other mental rehearsals, when you *anesthetize* pain, be sure to fill in details and involve as many of your five senses as possible as well as emotion.

Maybe your lower back is sore and the muscles feel as if they're in spasm. Zero in on your lower back. Picture a radio dial where the right side is pain and the left side is comfort. Fill in details. Feel the size of the knob and the grooves on it. What color is the knob? Hear the sound of the knob going click, click, click as you slowly rotate the dial counterclockwise away from the pain setting toward the comfort setting. Experience a sense of relief as your back feels progressively less painful until you're finally comfortable.

Another way I *anesthetize* pain is if I have a strained muscle, for example, I'll focus on the muscle and picture it looking red hot and like a tightly twisted towel. I imagine the pain subsiding as I visualize the color fading from red, to pink, to white. I watch the muscle gradually unwind until it changes from a twisted towel, to one that is hanging slack.

Kinesthetic and Auditory Imagery

To use imaging effectively, you need to do your mental rehearsal in a way that suits your particular learning style. Sixty-five to seventy-five percent of the population are *visual* thinkers. Twenty percent are *kinesthetic* learners in that they *feel* images in their bodies. The remaining ten percent are *auditory* learners; they translate much of their sensory experience into sound. To find out what kind of thinker you are, do the following exercise:

Think of a painful muscle as a tightly twisted towel, then anesthetize the pain by "seeing" the towel go slack.

Describe your barn. Does your description focus on the type of building and how the stalls, wash rack, and tack room are laid out? If so, you're probably a visual learner.

If, however, your emphasis is on the texture of the wood in the stalls and the coolness radiating up from the cement floor in the tack room, you're most likely a kinesthetic learner. If your focus is on the sounds of the horses munching hay in their stalls, the crunch of the gravel in the driveway under your feet, or the song of the barn swallows, you're an auditory learner.

All of us have a dominant sense backed up by a secondary sense. To visualize effectively, begin with your primary sense, then try to involve your other senses. As a kinesthetic learner, you can still use a *mental rehearsal* to enhance performance. In this case, however, make your images vivid by adding the sensations that you'd like to experience.

For example, maybe you have trouble sitting the trot. Remember what it felt like on the rare occasions that you sat the trot well. Perhaps you felt as if you were riding on an ocean wave. Or, maybe you felt as if your seat had dissolved into your horse's body. You felt the stickiness of your chaps or leather-seated breeches helping you stay in close contact with the saddle. You felt relaxed and in harmony with

Sitting the trot
well feels like
you're riding
along on the crest
of an ocean
wave.

your horse. Remember those feelings and re-create them as you practice your rides in your mind's eye.

If you're an auditory learner, focus on hearing your horse chewing softly on the bit, his rhythmic breathing, and the sound of his footfalls. How loud are those sounds? Are they muffled or clear? Are they regular or irregular? Is there anything unique about them? Do the sounds lull you into a state of relaxation?

Coping Rehearsal

I personally like to do *perfect practice*. Some of you, however, might find it difficult to do that type of rehearsal. No matter how hard you try to visualize desired results, negative pictures keep popping into your mind, and fighting to keep those negative images or thoughts out of your mind makes you feel anxious. Don't force the issue. Use *coping rehearsal* instead.

To use *coping rehearsal*, let the picture of the imagined disaster play out. For example, let's say you're mentally rehearsing a dressage test. The test says that you're to trot on a 20-meter circle at A going to the left. When you cross the centerline, you're supposed to pick up left-lead canter.

You've had problems picking up left-lead canter all week. Each time you asked, your horse threw his head up and over to the right, ran forward, and ended up on the wrong lead. At this point, even the thought of asking for left-lead canter makes you tense. You've been obsessing about this for several days and whenever you try to do your *perfect practice*, you always see your horse picking up the wrong lead when you're riding to the left.

Don't fight it. Go with it by using *coping rehearsal*. See yourself asking for left-lead canter. Watch your horse running headlong into the canter on the wrong lead. Don't stop there. Let yourself see the mistake in great detail, but then follow it through until you come out on the other side. See yourself staying organized in your position while you calmly bring your horse back to a rhythmic working trot. Reestablish the correct bend along the arc of the circle, and then quietly ask for the canter transition again. This time, see your horse calmly picking up a balanced left-lead canter.

You can also use *coping rehearsal* to help you with your emotions. Say, you're planning to bring your young horse to his very first clinic. He hasn't been to many new places, so you're afraid that he might be wild and you'll be catapulted into orbit. You keep seeing this potential disaster very clearly in your imagination, and you're very nervous.

Start your *mind's eye movie* as you arrive at the clinic's site. Take your horse off the trailer and observe him jigging, spinning, and generally working himself into a lather. When you prepare him for the lesson, notice how tight he is. As you put your foot in the stirrup, you feel as if he's ready to explode. Don't fight it. Just continue the scenario until you can "see" a successful resolution. Watch yourself as you go on a circle and pick up a slow, rhythmic working trot. Ignore the fact that in the beginning, your horse is "bouncing off the walls" and barely taking two steps in a row that are straight forward. Quietly continue to trot until he settles down. Notice how your respiration and heart rate remain normal and that you're not at all unseated by his antics. Within a few minutes, both of you are as relaxed and comfortable as you are at home.

Creating Your Own Perfect Practice Tape

Take advantage of the fact that visualizing a desired result in great detail eventually becomes your reality by putting together your own *perfect practice videotape*. For example, let's say you're struggling with a particular issue like jumping ditches. Make a tape of yourself riding over a ditch confidently and in perfect form. Edit your tape so that you show yourself taking the jump again and again. On one or two of the repetitions, play the clip in *slow motion*. Watch your tape as often as you

Make a *perfect practice tape* and watch it over and over again.

can to get a clear picture in your mind's eye of how you want to look and feel when you jump ditches.

I used this tool with Eastwood to help me when I was struggling with the canter "zigzag"—a series of half-passes where you half-pass in one direction, do a flying change, and then immediately half-pass back in the other direction. I had all kinds of challenges with this movement. Sometimes, I covered more ground sideways when I half-passed to the left than I did when I went to the right. Often, Woody would make a mistake in the flying change between the half-passes. Occasionally, his canter would get labored and the tempo would get too slow. More often than not, I didn't have an equal amount of bend through his body in both half-passes.

I asked a friend to tape my training sessions for a few days in a row. Over those days I managed to do the occasional good zigzag. Once I had one quality zigzag on tape, I took the tape home and edited together several repetitions of it. I repeated it in *slow motion*. When I was finished with my practice tape, it was about five minutes long. I watched that *perfect practice videotape* over and over, planting the right picture in my mind's eye. Within days, our zigzags improved dramatically.

Flash-Forward

Movies often use a flashback technique to take viewers from the present into the past. How about using a *flash-forward* technique to program your subconscious mind with desired results?

To use *flash-forward*, have both an image of yourself as you are now and an image of how you'd like to be. Perhaps right now you sit crookedly and collapse your waist to the right. This position fault has plagued you for years. Your goal is to sit straight and perfectly centered.

First, take three deep breaths to help you relax. Inhale deeply and exhale slowly. Hold the third deep breath for a count of ten, and as you exhale, feel yourself drifting into relaxation. Once you're relaxed, go ahead and picture yourself sitting crookedly, but don't put too much energy into this image. Then in two seconds or less, "whoosh" that image away. Replace it with a new, vibrant image of you sitting straight, centered, and in perfect balance. Fill in details on this second image. Ignite your senses:

- See how much taller you look when you sit up straight.
- Hear the rhythm of the footfalls.
- Smell the lilacs that are in bloom around the arena.
- Feel the even contact that both of your seat bones make with the saddle when you sit correctly.
- Add emotion to your image by reveling in the feeling of harmony you experience as you sit straight and balanced.

Improve your position by picturing yourself sitting crookedly, but don't put much energy into that image. Then, discard it, and substitute an image of your centered body in Technicolor.

Flash-forward five or six times from your present position to the position you would like to be in. A variation of the *flash-forward* technique is to picture your crooked position in black-and-white. Then, "whoosh" that picture away, and replace it with the image of your centered body in Technicolor. Go back and forth from black-and-white to color several times. Put very little energy and detail into the black-and-white image, but put lots of gusto and detail into the Technicolor image.[3]

Visualize your desired outcome as well as what you need to practice to achieve that goal.

Outcome and Process Imagery

Another interesting visualization technique is called *out-come and process imaging.* This type of imagery combines a picture of the final goal with one of the process by which the goal is achieved.

For example, your *outcome image* might show your horse with a blue ribbon on his bridle. Your *process image* might show you practicing the various movements in a "perfect" dressage test. Or, your outcome might be to jump with as much style and finesse as Anne Kursinski, while your process image shows you developing your skills by jumping gymnastics.[4]

Anne Kursinski
and Eros

Even More Essentials for Visualization

- Use a *zoom lens* to zero in on a part of your body or your horse's body.
- If you can't visualize yourself conquering a riding problem, *borrow a professional's body or his horse.*
- *You're the director* of your *mind's eye movies.* Be creative. Use different camera angles and *slow motion.*
- Use visualization to *anesthetize* pain.
- Modify your *mental rehearsal* to suit your personal learning style. If you're a *kinesthetic* or *auditory* learner, focus on how things *feel* or *sound.*
- If you find *perfect practice* effortful, do *coping rehearsal* instead.
- Make a *perfect practice videotape* that highlights the results you want.
- Use *flash-forward* to get you from where you are to where you want to be.
- Do *outcome and process imagery* by alternating your mental pictures between the desired final result and the steps you need to go through to achieve that result.

20

Distraction

One of the biggest challenges that riders face is staying focused. Sometimes, we get distracted when there's a lot of activity going on around us, when we're insecure and worried about what others are thinking, when we get preoccupied by personal issues, when we're afraid that our horse is going to be too fresh, when we're tense and can't relax enough to concentrate, or when we're not in harmony and are frustrated with our horse.

To ride and train successfully, your horse needs you to stay *in the moment* and concentrate on what you're doing. If you don't concentrate, he certainly won't. For those of you who compete, you need to be able to block out all kinds of distractions including the other competitors, the spectators, loose animals, and the voices of trainers coaching other people. Fortunately, concentration is a skill and there are many tools to help develop it.

In Chapter 9, I discussed brain waves and explained how the ideal for visualizing is a low Alpha/borderline Theta state. In this state, the oscillations of your brain waves are approximately 7 to 9 per second, and you feel deeply relaxed. The ideal for concentration is a low Beta/borderline Alpha state. In this state the oscillations of your brain waves are approximately 12 to 14 per second, and you're more alert yet still relaxed. If you have trouble focusing when you ride or compete, it probably means that you're in a Beta state with brain-wave activity at approximately 14 to 40 per second. This is too fast to be able to concentrate effectively.[1]

The solution, therefore, is to slow down brain-wave activity. You can do this through any number of techniques, such as listening to soothing music, meditation, or yoga to name a few. You can also use any of the relaxation exercises I discussed in Chapter 9: *progressive relaxation*; *autogenic relaxation*; *sonic meditation*; *scanning*; *belly breathing*; *plus/minus signs*; *deep relaxation*; *the centaur; click the pen*; and *squeeze the sponge*.

Build Your Concentration Muscles

One of my students, Dinah, had a real challenge staying focused for any length of time. Dinah was the type of person whose mind was always in fast-forward. She knew this personality trait was interfering with her riding, so we came up with a plan to *build her concentration muscles.*

I told Dinah to think of developing her ability to concentrate in the same way that she'd develop physical strength. In other words, if her goal was to get stronger physically, she'd alternate periods of stressing her muscles with periods of recovery—if she embarked on a weight-training program at the gym, one day she'd exercise a particular muscle group like her legs, for example, and the next day she'd allow the muscles of her legs to recover and she'd work her chest and arms instead. She wouldn't work the same muscle group two days in a row. A program like this works because muscles don't get stronger during periods of stress. They get stronger during rest when they're allowed to recover. I explained to Dinah that she could *build her concentration muscles* in the same way that she could strengthen the rest of the muscles in her body—by alternating periods of intense concentration with periods of complete relaxation.

We began with her position. I told her to focus fully and intently on her body for a few moments as she rode around the ring. She was to go through a position checklist. She started with her head. She made sure her eyes were up and her head was in line with her upper body. Next, she moved to her neck. Was it relaxed? Then, she thought about her chest and shoulders. Was her chest open, and were her shoulders back and down? She gradually worked her way down to her feet then took a break. She walked around on a loose rein for a few minutes and allowed her mind to wander. Then, she picked up the reins again and repeated the whole procedure.

Next, she went through the same process during an exercise with her horse. We started with a leg-yield in the trot. The plan was for Dinah to ask her horse to move away from her right leg over to the left. As he stepped sideways, she was to focus on what he was doing by running through a checklist of the ingredients that make up a good leg-yield in the trot:

- *Rhythm:* Was the beat of the trot a regular one-two, one-two, one-two rhythm?
- *Tempo:* Was the tempo a comfortable speed—neither too fast nor too slow?
- *Straightness:* Was her horse's body straight? Was his neck lined up absolutely in front of his body? She flexed him at the poll to the right, away from the direction he was traveling, while she kept his neck straight.
- *Alignment:* Was her horse's body almost parallel to the track but with his forehand ever so slightly in advance? In this position, his front legs would meet the track just a moment before his hind legs.
- *Responsiveness:* Did her horse move sideways willingly from a light leg aid, or did she feel like she had to use a lot of leg pressure?
- *Body position:* Was she thinking about sitting to the left as he went sideways so her shoulders stayed square and her weight stayed over the center of the horse? Or, was her upper body leaning to the right as she was left behind the movement? Were her hands side-by-side, or was she pulling backward on the right rein—the rein that she used to ask for flexion?

Work your way through your mental checklist, take a break and walk on a loose rein, then have another go at it.

Once she had run through her checklist during one or two leg-yields, she took a break by walking on a loose rein. After she had relaxed a bit, she picked up the reins and had another go at it. By doing this type of exercise, little by little she increased her ability to focus fully for longer periods of time.

Interestingly enough, this is the same approach you would use when teaching a young horse to focus on his work. Not only do you start with very short periods of intense concentration and give him frequent breaks, but you also keep the entire session very short—perhaps fifteen to twenty minutes. Then, you gradually build up the length of time he has to concentrate between breaks as well as the overall length of your session.

Role-Playing

I introduced *role-playing* to you in Chapter 12, *Doubt* (p. 112). You can use *role-playing* when you're having trouble staying focused.

My friend, Sue Blinks, happens to be my role model for focus and concentration. I've never seen anyone get into "focus mode" the way she does. I often joke with her that a bomb could go off near the arena, and she probably wouldn't hear it. (In fact, to test my theory about her concentration skills, I once placed a two-foot high, plastic, orange pumpkin smack dab in the middle of her arena to see how long it would take her to notice it. It took her several laps around the ring before she saw it!)

When I'm having one of those "completely distracted" days and my mind is going in a hundred different directions, I pretend I'm Sue. To do my *role-playing*, I put on Sue's "game face" and mimic her working attitude. In minutes, I'm transported into a *cocoon of concentration*.

Distraction to Concentration

- The ideal state for concentration is a low Beta/borderline Alpha state. If you have trouble concentrating, you need to slow down your brain-wave activity by doing *relaxation* exercises.
- *Build your concentration muscles* by alternating periods of intense concentration with periods of total relaxation.
- To move yourself from distraction to concentration, do some *role-playing*.

21

Coping with Fear

Riders at all levels of experience seem to struggle with fear. People tell me they often go to tremendous lengths to stay in their *comfort zone* so they can avoid the dry-mouthed, sweaty-palmed, and rubber-legged symptoms of fear. Since fear is such a huge issue for many riders, I'm going to devote an entire chapter to it here. First, I'll discuss how you can manage fear through mental training; then I'll show you how you can feel more secure by training your horse to be a safer mount.

Recognizing Fear

Fear can express itself in many different ways. It can disguise itself as worry, anxiety, insecurity, timidity, obsession, or doubt. It invades our lives as fear of failure, fear of physical injury, fear of embarrassment, fear of helplessness, and even fear of success.

Riders often beat themselves up about being fearful. I have students who call themselves "self-proclaimed chickens," or "gutless wonders." I try to explain to them that, in fact, they're incredibly brave. After all, courage isn't the absence of fear. If you're not at least a little afraid when you tackle certain jumps on the cross-country course, move up to a higher level of competition, or put yourself on the line in any number of ways, then bravery isn't even the issue. It's only when you're nervous and take a risk *in spite of your fear,* that you're truly courageous.

Recently, I was at a party and my sister-in-law asked me if I had ever been afraid during the course of my career. I laughed at her question and told her that I was afraid much of the time. Every time I tackle a project like a new book or tape series, do a spot on television, give a speech in front of hundreds of people, get on an airplane, compete at a big show, or coach at an important event like the Olympics, I am afraid to one degree or another. But, I also told her that I didn't think being afraid was such a big deal. Although fear has been my companion throughout my career, it has never stopped me from doing what I want to do. Because I challenge and stretch myself in spite of my fears, I consider myself very brave. It certainly would be a lot easier to stay in my *comfort zone*. But I take the risk. Doing what I want to do *in spite of my fear* is precisely what makes me courageous.

My philosophy of pushing through fear was really put to the test after the terrorist attacks on the United States on September 11, 2001. Like the rest of the country, I was numbed by the monstrous events of that day. To add to my horror, a close member of my family was a passenger on the first plane that was flown into the World Trade Center.

Shortly after the attacks, I was scheduled to do a seminar in Montana. Even though I was afraid to fly, I resolved to continue to live normally and still planned on going. Then, two days before I was to leave, a government report was issued saying that there was an imminent threat of another attack that week. The information apparently came from "reliable sources."

My resolve faltered. I agonized for the next twenty-four hours about whether or not I should get on a plane to make the flight across the country. I was definitely leaning toward tucking my tail between my legs and staying home.

I sent an email to my publisher and friend, Caroline Robbins, to ask her advice. I call Caroline "the voice of reason" because she always seems to have her two feet planted firmly on the ground. She wisely advised me that there was a fine line between fear and terror. She said, "You must decide, but I feel that we have to live our lives as normally as possible, because fear today could become terror tomorrow. It is easier to face fear than terror."

As usual, she was right. When I got on the plane in Boston for the trek across the country, I was quite panicked. But once I did it, I was hugely relieved and managed to fly home without giving my fears more than a passing thought.

By flying in spite of my fear, I was able to prevent the fear from growing into a paralyzing monster.

Fear Becomes the Goal

Remember, your subconscious mind doesn't make value judgments. It doesn't care if the goal you give it is positive or negative. It just gives you what it thinks you want, sending you as if you're a *guided missile* toward your current *dominant thought*. If your language and mental pictures focus on your fears, those fears become the target, and therefore, reality.

For example, if you repeatedly say, "My horse isn't ready for this level and my ride is going to be a disaster," or "I'm a basket case when I compete and can't sleep at all the night before," or "I'm afraid my horse will have a mental 'meltdown' if I ask for more collection," the words, "disaster," "basket case," and "meltdown," become certainties.

Maybe you don't express your fears out loud, but you're gifted with an extremely vivid imagination (translation—you worry a lot). You're a master at picturing potential disaster in great detail, like the rider who told me she had a very vivid mental image of what would happen when she took her young horse to his first show. She clearly "saw" him launching her into the air where she did a perfect full-twisting somersault before landing flat on her face in the dirt!

When you visualize scenes like this in vivid living color, they become fact. Picture landing flat on your face in the dirt, and it's more likely you will land flat on your face in the dirt! I realize it's inevitable that when you're afraid, pictures pop into your mind. However, do a *pattern interrupt*, and prevent those frightening pictures from becoming the goal.

Thought Stopping

I introduced the concept of *thought stopping* to you in *That Winning Feeling!* Here's a quick review, and an example of how you can use this tool to help you deal with fear.

When you find yourself visualizing imminent disaster, break your pattern by doing some *thought stopping* right away. As soon as the alarming picture pops into your head, use an action word to quiet your mind and erase it. Your action word might be something like: "Clear," "Focus," "Stop!" "Relax," "Let go," or "Breathe."

Once you've done some *thought stopping*, replace the negative thought with a positive one. This is an important step, because if you don't fill your mind with a positive thought, the negative picture will creep right back in. So, as soon as you've interrupted the negative thought with an action word, reprogram your mental computer.

Visualization and Self-Talk

Here's an example of doing some *thought stopping* and then using visualization and self-talk to *change your software*. You're getting ready to start your young horse under saddle. You've raised him since he was a baby and you've been looking forward to this moment. You've prepared him thoroughly by getting him used to the tack, teaching him how to longe, and basic voice commands. Everything is going according to plan, but about a week before, you start to get cold feet. Your imagination goes into overdrive.

You've seen your youngster buck on the longe line and you know how athletic he is. Now you "see" him bucking exuberantly as soon as you settle into the saddle. Your legs turn to jelly and your mouth is dry. You "feel" yourself being tossed about like a rag doll until finally you part company and end up on the ground. Your self-talk becomes, "Am I nuts? I'm a thirty-seven-year-old mother of two children. I can't afford to get hurt on a young horse."

When your imagination starts running wild like this, first do some *thought stopping*. Say, "Clear," or "Stop it!" Next, *replace* that pessimistic picture with a *mind's eye movie* of you and your young horse going through your first ride quietly, calmly and successfully. Make sure you fill in details, involve your senses and add emotion to your movie.

If you're overwhelmed by your fears and find yourself struggling to picture a calm scene, do some *coping rehearsal* instead (p. 170). Rather than worrying that you're going to be catapulted into the air, do the following. "Watch" the disaster unfold, "see" it in great detail, but then continue your *mind's eye movie* until you see a *successful resolution*.

For example, "see" yourself and an assistant preparing your horse for his first session under saddle. Your assistant holds your youngster with the longe line as you "belly" him by lying over the saddle. He seems okay with this, so you swing your right leg over. You feel a hump in his back so you take your time and pat him all over so he can get used to you being above him. When he relaxes, your assistant leads him forward a step. At that moment, he gets frightened and shoots forward. When he shoots forward, he startles himself. His tail goes straight up in the air like a flag and he begins to buck dramatically.

At this point, do a *coping rehearsal* by continuing your *mind's eye movie* until you have a happy ending. Despite your horse's antics, you recognize that you're never actually unseated. Your breathing stays fairly normal and your physical tension gradually dissolves. After those initial exciting moments, your youngster settles down. He soon realizes you're not a cougar who has jumped on his back. He begins to listen to your voice, relaxes, and carries you around as if he's had a rider on his back all his life.

The next part of *changing your software* is to use empowering self-talk. Find *buzzwords* that strengthen you. Maybe your words for the situation I've just described will be something like, "relaxed and attentive." Or, perhaps you'll choose "calm, confident, capable."

One of my students froze every time she thought her horse was going to wheel around and take off in the opposite direction. Her catch phrase became, "Take charge," and that mobilized her. Another rider, who tended to be too cautious in competition, used the phrase, "I'm a risk-taker." Yet another rider found she could let go of tight muscles by saying, "My butt is like a marshmallow!"

A Positive Attitude toward Fear

Another way to look at fear is to give yourself an *attitude adjustment*. In Chapter 15, page 127, I talked a lot about the importance of attitude. Not only does having the right attitude help you reach your goals, but, having a *winning attitude* can actually help you deal with fear.

One way you can give yourself an *attitude adjustment* is to adopt an *attitude of gratitude* (see p. 131). Think about it. Rather than focusing on what you're afraid

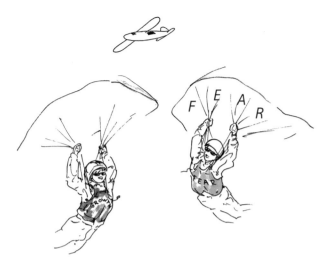

Think of fear as a companion that accompanies you on all your adventures.

Consider fear a green light to go ahead and move out of your comfort zone.

of, focus on what you're grateful for. Remind yourself how lucky you are to be able to spend time outdoors with these beautiful animals. You're so fortunate to experience the friendship and joy that horses bring into your life. Be grateful that you're healthy enough at this moment in your life to be able to ride.

When you start to get overwhelmed by fear, remember these two little words—"thank you." Thank you for giving me the gift of horses. Thank you for giving me the gift of riding. Thank you for giving me the mental capacity and physical ability to enjoy this sport.

Remember, no situation is inherently good or bad. It's up to you to choose how you're going to react to events. Let's apply that concept to fear. Consider the possibility that fear itself really isn't the problem. In fact, in many cases you can look at fear positively. It's a symptom of growth. Every time you stretch yourself, aim a little higher, or take a risk, you're growing. And when you're growing, you're going to have some anxiety. It's only natural, because you're stepping outside your *comfort zone*. So fear itself is not the issue. Fear is part of our survival mechanism—it's a signal to take action. The problem exists only when your fear is out of proportion to the situation or it immobilizes you.

Rather than interpreting fear as a signal to retreat, think of it as a "green light" to move ahead. After all, if fear goes hand-in-hand with growth, why would you want to get rid of it completely? Instead, look at fear as a sign of your development, and recognize fear as a companion that accompanies you on all your adventures.[1]

Interestingly enough, as you use that "green light" to signal you to take action, you'll find that doing something actually decreases your fear and makes it more manageable. You see, you might think you're safe if you stay in your *comfort zone*. But refusing to push through your fears actually makes you feel worse. That's because you end up feeling helpless on top of everything else. So, push through your fears by taking a small risk every day. I'm not saying that you should take foolish chances. Always make sure you're well prepared for the task at hand. But taking a well-thought-out risk will make you feel great. And even if it doesn't work out, at least you've made an effort. You're not sitting back immobilized by your fears.

What If?

When dealing with fear, your self-talk is generally negative. It usually takes the form of *"What if?"* questions. Your inner dialogue might sound something like, "What if I forget my test?" "What if I go off course?" "What if I fall off?" "What if my horse bolts when he sees a deer?" "What if I make a fool of myself in front of all those people?"

You can deal with these "What if?" questions in two stages. First, preface every "What if?" with the word, *"So."* In other words, "What if I go off course?" becomes "So what if I go off course?" "What if I fall off?" becomes, "So what if I fall off?"

The second part of dealing with "What if?" questions is to say *"I can handle it,"* right after you say *"So what if?"* After all, if you truly believe that you can handle anything, you have nothing to fear. Your new motto becomes, *"I can handle it."* The bottom line is that you *can* and *will* handle it. You have no other choice.[2]

Here are some examples of how you can use this sort of positive self-talk to help you deal with your fears:

If your niggling, undermining, fearful, conscious mind says, "What if I make a fool of myself in front of all those people?" You answer by saying, "So what if I make a fool of myself in front of all those people? I can handle it."

When your insecure conscious mind replies, "Yeah, but what if they laugh at me?" You answer by saying. "So what if they laugh at me? I can handle it."

You're taking your young horse out for his first solo trail ride. You're having a fine time enjoying the scenery and then for no particular reason, the negative self-talk starts. You say to yourself, "What if a deer jumps out of the woods, and my horse bolts? Answer, "So what if he runs off? I can handle it. He has to stop eventually."

This two-step process of adding, "So," to your, "What if?" question and answering with an, "I can handle it," can help you cope with many situations that scare you. This technique works because the truth is, you CAN handle it.

Stay in the Moment

When you're fearful, your mind isn't on what's happening right now, it is on what might happen in the future. Most of what you're afraid of never comes to pass. Why use up so much energy and emotion worrying about things that might happen but usually never do? Instead, keep your fear manageable by *staying in the moment.*

CASE HISTORY

Sarah

Sarah wrote to me about having such a bad experience on her first horse that her fear prevented her from enjoying her new horse. She told me that she began riding several years ago, and her first horse figured out very quickly that she was a beginner. He learned that he could easily scare her by bucking her off at the canter. She explained:

"With much help from my trainer, I learned to sit his vicious bucks and twists. But, when I managed those, he came up with more nasty tricks. After five long years, I gave up. I gave him back to his breeder. I was afraid that if I sold him, he would hurt someone. I was so dejected that I gave up riding for a while.

"After a three-year hiatus, I began riding a very gentle Quarter horse. This horse never made a wrong move and was very forgiving. But, because of my experiences with the first horse, the thought of cantering frightened me terribly. In lessons, I would canter a circle once and then start thinking something was going to happen to me—as it had so many times in the past. My teacher and I tried everything, but I was still afraid."

I helped Sarah work through her fear by teaching her how to *stay in the moment.* Each time she felt herself worrying about what might happen, I told her to bring her attention back to the present. She achieved this in a number of ways.

> To hold your fear at bay, train yourself to stay in the moment by concentrating on your immediate surroundings.

Smell those lilacs. Hear those birds. Feel the warmth of that sun!

One thing she did was to look at her immediate surroundings. She noticed the horses turned out in nearby pastures, the fence around her ring, the tree line in the distance, or other riders. She also involved her senses. She smelled the fragrance of lilacs that were blooming near the arena. She listened to birds chirping, or the rhythmic breathing of her horse. She focused on the feeling of her legs around her horse's body. She imagined that her legs were molded to her horse's sides the way a wet towel would drape around and cling to his barrel.

Sarah also used *buzzwords* to *stay in the moment*. When her mind started to wander, she'd say, "Focus!" or, "This is fun!" or, "I love this!" to bring herself back to the present.

I'm pleased to report that by learning to *stay in the moment*, she now canters happily. In fact, she says she just can't canter enough!

Bargain with Your Fear

Perhaps it better suits your personality to use self-talk to *bargain with your fear*. For instance, you might say something like this. "Just leave me alone and give me a few minutes of peace so I can warm up this three-year-old (jump this fence, run those barrels, ride this test, or work this cow) and then I'll pay attention to you again."

In *That Winning Feeling!* I suggested that you *bargain with your fears* by putting a time limit on obsessing about them. During that specified time, worry your head off. Pour your heart and soul into agonizing about your fears. Then, when your time is up, put your worries aside. If you begin to worry at any other time during the day, tell your fears they'll just have to wait until your designated "worry time" the next day before you can pay attention to them again.

Picture What You Want

Since you can only concentrate on one thing at a time, think about what you *want* rather than what you don't want. Instead of repeating, "Don't buck," or, "Don't shy," focus on something you want instead. Remember, there's no picture in the mind for the word "not."

Imagine your horse staying steadily on the bit and say the word "round" over and over. Feel an elastic contact with his mouth and say, "Soft and supple, soft and

Concentrate on what you want, not on what you are afraid will happen.

supple." By doing so, you fill your mind with what you want rather than with what you don't want.

Setting the Stage for Safety

Basically, to feel safe you need to know you can stop, go, slow down, and steer. You'll be much less fearful and a lot more confident if you're well prepared. Being prepared includes training your horse intelligently. Specifically, you need to be able to communicate clearly so your horse knows exactly what you want him to do. You teach him one signal (cue) at a time, and give such precise aids that he doesn't get confused, and you can easily have a conversation with him. The more you can have a meaningful dialogue with your horse, the safer you'll feel. In the next section, I'll look at some of the things you can do to make your horse more reliable.

Voice Commands on a Lead Line

To start building your confidence, let's make your horse safe by teaching him some basic voice commands. You need a halter, a lead line with a chain, and a long whip about 44 inches long. Put on the halter so its noseband is about 2 inches below the horse's cheekbones, and attach the lead line as follows starting on the left side of the head:

Thread the snap on the chain downward through the lower left ring of the halter.

Lift the chain up so it crosses over the noseband of the halter but not so the chain directly presses on the horse's face.

Feed it out and up through the lower right halter ring.

Attach the snap of the chain to the upper right ring of the halter.

Make sure the snap is away from your horse's face. If it rubs, it can come undone.

You will need 4 to 6 inches of chain on the left side to work with. If you are left with more (the chain is too long), pull the snap through the upper right ring, and attach it back on the chain (figs. 1 to 3).[3]

Hold the lead line with your right hand about 8 to 10 inches from the halter (fig. 4). Layer the excess lead line in your left hand. Never wind the excess lead around your hand because you could be injured if your horse becomes startled and suddenly pulls away (figs. 5 and 6).

Before you start these leading lessons, take some time to get your horse used to the whip. Quietly rub it all over his body until he stands quietly when he feels it (fig. 7). Once your horse is comfortable with the whip, you'll be able to use it as an aid. Carry the whip in your left hand along with the excess lead line.

When leading your horse, the correct position for your body is just in front of his shoulder. He should neither be walking too far in front of you nor dragging behind you (fig. 8).

Your goal with this groundwork is to train your horse to react *immediately* to simple voice commands to stop, go, and slow down. Horses learn by association, so, in the beginning, combine a voice commands with three additional cues.

The first cue will be the movement of your body. When you want him to go forward, you start walking. When you want him to slow down, you slow down. When you want him to stop, you stop.

The other two cues are use of the lead line and the whip. Use the lead line to help stop him. And, depending on where you use it on his body, you can use the whip to tell him to stop or to move forward.

Begin by going from the halt to the walk. From your position at his shoulder, take a step forward, reach behind your waist and touch him with the whip on his barrel where your leg rests (fig. 9). As you take a step and touch him, say, "Walk on," in an energetic voice. As soon as he walks forward, reward him by praising him with your voice, or patting him.

Walk forward a few steps and then say, "Whoa," or "Ho," in a slow, soothing voice. As you give the verbal cue, stop walking. If he continues to walk forward,

1. Thread the snap on the chain down through the halter's lower left ring.

2. Take the chain across and on top of noseband. Feed it through the lower right ring.

3. Attach snap to the upper right ring away from the horse's face.

4. With the right hand, hold the lead line 8 to 10 inches from the halter.

5. Layer any excess lead line in the left hand.

6. Never wind excess lead line around the hand.

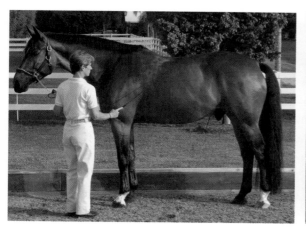

7. To encourage the horse to be comfortable with the whip, rub it over his body.

8. Lead the horse just in front of his shoulder.

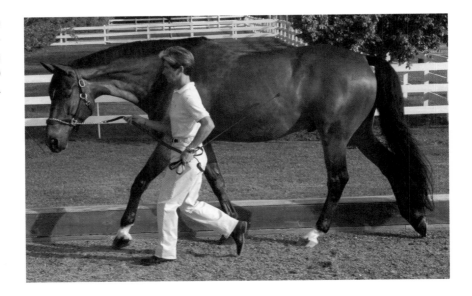

9. Touch the whip on the horse's barrel where your leg goes to ask him to go forward.

lift the whip in front of his face (fig. 10). If he still doesn't stop, touch him on the chest with the top of the whip, and apply a take-and-give pressure on his nose with the chain (fig. 11). If he still walks forward, give a couple of sharp tugs on the chain. As soon as he stops, praise him with your voice, or pat him.

The next stage is to get a prompt reaction to your voice without the extra cues. Eliminate the movement of your body as an extra cue, first. Try saying, "Walk on," and "Whoa;" use the whip and the lead rope to help only if necessary. Don't move or stop until he does.

When he does this easily, eliminate the lead and the whip as aids. Ask your horse to walk forward and to "whoa" solely from your voice command. When he does, make a huge fuss over him. Pat him, praise him verbally, and give him a treat. If he stops reacting promptly to your voice, add one of your additional cues back in until you get a response. Then, go back to just using your voice again.

Go through these same steps with transitions from walk to trot and back to walk, as well as halt to trot and back to halt. Your verbal cue for trotting can be a brisk, "Terrrot." Use the added cues of your body movement, whip, and lead line as needed, but remember that your ultimate goal is to get your horse to halt, walk, and trot solely from your voice.

10. If the horse continues to walk, despite a verbal cue to stop, lift the whip up in front of his face.

11. If he still does not stop, touch him on the chest with the top of the whip and apply a take-and-give pressure on his nose.

Once he can halt, walk, and trot on the lead like this, teach your horse to slow down *within* his gait. The same rules apply. Start by combining a voice command such as "Slow," or "Steady," with your body movement, the lead line, and the whip.

For example, start with an animated walk. Say, "Slow," as you apply a bit of pressure on his nose and slow down your own walk. If he doesn't react to these aids, give some sharp tugs on the lead. Once he slows down, praise him.

To return to the animated walk, say, "Walk on," as you touch him on his barrel with the whip and speed up your own walk.[4]

Voice Commands on a Longe Line

When you've established these basic verbal cues on the lead line, do them on the longe line. For information on the equipment you need to longe and how to adjust it correctly, see the *Appendix* (p. 217) for a brief summary of the information that first appeared in Chapter Four of my book, *Cross-Train Your Horse: Simple Dressage for Every Horse, Every Sport.*

Go through the same steps on the longe line that you did when you were leading your horse. In the beginning, combine the verbal command with the position of your body, the longe line, and the whip.

When longeing, a neutral position of your body is at the horse's girth area so that there is a triangle formed between your body, the longe line, your horse's body,

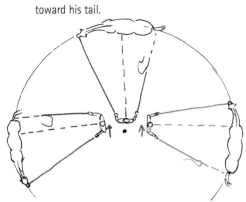

12. When longeing, your neutral body position is standing at the horse's girth area. To slow the horse down, move toward his head. To drive him forward, move toward his tail.

and the whip. When you want to slow your horse down with your body position, move laterally toward his head so that you're positioned more in front of him. When you want to drive him forward, step laterally toward his hind end. In other words, if he is facing and traveling to the left, step to the left to slow him down, and to the right to speed him up (fig. 12). In addition, use sharp tugs on the longe line to slow him down or snap the whip toward his hind legs to drive him forward.

Review all the voice commands that you introduced in your leading lessons. Then, add cantering to

his vocabulary. To differentiate the sound of this command, you might say some-
thing like, "Aaannnnndddd
canter," or, "Canter, hup!"

When you are longe-
ing, your goal is the same
as it was with the lessons
on the lead line—to eliminate having to use your
body, tugs on the line, and
whip. You want to be able
to halt, walk, trot, canter,
and slow down from your
voice alone.

Next, it's time for
your horse to associate the
voice commands he learned during the groundwork to this new work under saddle. If you need, start with an assistant who can either lead or longe you.

Voice Commands When Riding

Go through the same steps while mounted that you did when you were on the
ground. This time, however, when you give the voice command, combine it with
an aid from your body. For instance, when you say, "Walk on," or "Terrot," close
both calves. When you say, "Aannnnddd canter," squeeze with your inside leg on
the girth as you swing your outside leg a couple of inches behind the girth in a
windshield wiper-like action. Your leg aids should be very light. If your horse does-
n't react in an energetic and enthusiastic way to a light aid, give him a sharp kick
with both legs to wake him up (fig. 13). Then go back and retest with a polite aid.

When you say, "Whoa," or "Slow," close your hands (figs. 14 A & B) and "still"
your seat by keeping your upper body vertical and your shoulders down and back while
you contract your stomach muscles, so that your hips stop following your horse's

13. When the horse
does not react to
your aids in an ener-
getic manner, give
him a sharp kick
with both legs to
wake him up.

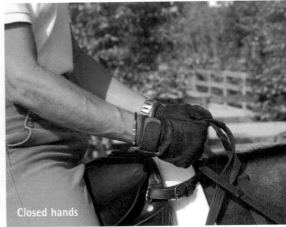

Neutral hands | Closed hands

14 A and B When you say "Whoa," close your hands and....

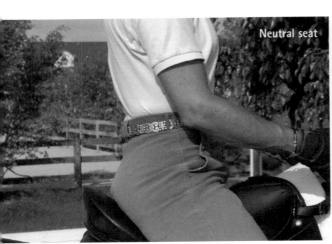

Neutral seat | "Stilled" seat

15 A and B ... "still" your seat by contracting the stomach muscles. Notice how this action takes so|
curve out of the small of the back.

motion (figs. 15 A & B). The degree and duration of closing your hands and "stilling" your seat tells your horse whether he's to merely slow down or if he's to stop completely. If you use your hands and seat like this and your horse ignores you, bring him sharply to the halt with your reins. Then, once you've corrected him, go back and ask him to slow down or stop from the more subtle aid.

When you feel confident that you can get your horse to stop, go, and slow down on command, you are better prepared and will feel more secure about being able to communicate with him.

"Steering" on the Ground

The next confidence-building skill is the ability to steer. You begin this work on the ground as well.

The biggest mistake a rider makes when she is having trouble steering or turning is to pull her horse's head in the direction she wants to go (fig. 16) This doesn't work because you can pull on your horse's face as hard as you like, but if he's determined to go the other way, his body will go in that direction regardless of where he's looking. The key to steering your horse is the ability to control his shoulders. When you can move your horse's shoulders left or right, the rest of his body will follow.

16. The biggest mistake many riders make when they have steering troubles is to pull the horse's head in the direction the rider wants to go. You can pull on your horse's face as hard as you can, but his body can still go in the direction he chooses. The key is to be able to move his shoulders.

I call the exercises that follow "shoulder-reining" exercises. Start from the ground at the halt. Hold the lead line in your left hand. Use your right hand to push on your horse's left shoulder. When he yields away from this pressure and moves his shoulders to the right, praise him (fig. 17).

Now go to the right side of his body. Hold the lead in your right hand, and use your left hand to push on his right shoulder. Praise him when he moves his shoulder away from the pressure.

Go back on the left side and walk forward. Every ten steps or so, give a little push on his shoulder to get him to move his shoulder over to the right (fig. 18). Do the same thing from the other side.

Once you can move your horse's shoulders when you're on the ground, start to "shoulder-rein" him while mounted.

18. Every ten steps or so give a little push to ask the horse to move his shoulder over.

17. Shoulder-reining exercise on the *ground:* Use the right hand to push on the horse's left shoulder and vice versa.

"Steering" on the Horse

The first step in the mounted, "shoulder-reining" process is to position your horse's face away from the direction you want to move his shoulders. This positioning is called "flexion at the poll." You flex him to the left (fig. 19) if you want to move his shoulders to the right, and flex him to the right if you want to move his shoulders to the left.

19. Shoulder-reining exercise on the *horse:* Flex the horse to the left to move his shoulders to the right, and vice versa. This positioning is called "flexion at the poll."

20. Ask for "flexion at the poll" by vibrating one rein. Hold the opposite rein firmly so the horse doesn't bend his entire neck.

Ask for flexion by vibrating (or squeezing and releasing, or moving your wrist like you scramble eggs) the rein. As you vibrate one rein, hold the opposite rein firmly. If you don't support with the opposite rein, you won't be able to isolate his poll. Instead, your horse will end up bending his entire neck (fig. 20).

Start by traveling to the right in the walk. The plan is to make a square with four corners. Flex your horse at the poll to the left. When you're ready to turn his shoulders in the corner, keep your hands side-by-side and move both of them in the

direction of the turn, which in this case, is to the right. Your right hand is used as an opening (or leading) rein, while your left hand gives an indirect rein aid (fig. 21).

During the indirect rein aid, your left hand comes as close to the withers as possible without ever actually crossing over them. For a horse whose shoulders are really stuck, you'll need a little leverage, so think of "knocking," "spinning," or "sliding" your horse's shoulders around the turn with a quick movement of your two arms. As you work your way around the turn, "shoulder-rein" him over with this quick but smooth action with both arms, and then soften the contact for a second. Then, "shoulder-rein" him again, and soften again (figs. 22 A & B). If your horse's shoulders still feel "stuck" and

21. To turn the horse's shoulders in a corner, keep your hands side by side, and move both in the direction of the turn.

he's hard to turn, bring your left leg forward, and while you're using your reins, give him little nudge with your foot up by his shoulder. If he still feels hard to turn, bring your weight sharply to the right as you use your reins and left leg in the way I've just described.

Your ultimate goal is to get your horse to turn from your reins alone—without having to knock him off balance with your body weight, or having to use your left leg near his shoulder. You'll know you have complete control over your horse's shoulders when you can use your reins as I've described and the contact with his mouth doesn't get heavier. The weight of the reins should stay exactly the same before, during and after the turn. In the beginning, when you go to turn, you'll feel a substantial increase in the weight of the reins. As your horse starts to turn better, the weight in your hands will be less. Eventually, there will be no increase in the weight of the reins: If you have one pound in each hand before you turn, you'll have one pound in each hand as you slide your horse's shoulders around the turn.

22 A and B
To "slide" the horse's shoulders around a turn, "shoulder-rein" him with a quick but smooth movement of the arms, and then soften the contact for a second.

In an Emergency

So far in this chapter, I've concentrated on the kind of fear that expresses itself as worry, anxiety, insecurity or doubt. I'm now going to focus on the fear of getting hurt. First, remember that much of what we're afraid of—falling off, for example—rarely happens. On the few occasions we do get dumped, we rarely get badly hurt. Yet, so many riders obsess about falling off and getting seriously hurt. How much fun can you have if you spend a lot of time worrying about what might happen next? What you need are the tools and the riding ability to deal with a horse that bucks, rears, bolts, or shies. Armed with these skills, you should feel much better prepared and, therefore, much more relaxed.

Most of the scary things that horses do to us are caused by instinctive behaviors. Rationally, you might understand that these behaviors exist to preserve the species and keep it safe from predators—unfortunately, that's little comfort when you're sitting on a horse that resists in a frightening manner.

Rearing

Of all of the expressions of resistance, rearing is one of the most serious. It's potentially dangerous because the horse can lose his balance and flip over. (Because of the serious nature of this problem, you might consider professional help to sort it out.)

There are many possible reasons for rearing. Below, I elaborate and give you some simple suggestions you can use to possibly avoid rearing in some cases. It's important to be aware of reasons for rearing so you can do everything in your power to prevent your horse from doing so in the first place. If he does rear in spite of your efforts, I will show you how to sit, and how to correct your horse.

Some of the most common causes of rearing include:

Extreme fright

Body soreness

Harsh bit

Tension

Frustration caused by confusion or fatigue

Rider's "rude" hands

Rider's unreasonable requests for collection

Non-acceptance of the aids

Unwillingness to accept contact

Extreme fright: Try not to put your horse in a situation where he's overfaced, such as jumping fences that are too big for him, or threatened—some horses get frightened if they're in a crowded warm-up area, with other horses coming straight at them.

Body soreness: Liase with your vet. Know if your horse is trying to cope with pain from a sore back, hocks, hips or legs, or teeth that need floating.

Harsh bit: Get a milder bit. And, make sure the new bit is the right thickness. Some horses have a thicker tongue and low palate, so a thinner bit—usually considered less mild—might actually be more comfortable for him.

Tension: Do some exercises that help your horse relax. (See Chapter Eleven on *Suppling for Balance and Harmony* in *Cross-Train Your Horse*.)

Frustration from confusion: Be sure to explain your horse's work to him in a logical, systematic way. Always lay a solid foundation for new work so that you can build on it, and keep resistance to a minimum. Make sure your seat is independent enough so that you don't give conflicting aids where your legs say, "Go," while your hands are pulling, saying, "Stop."

Frustration from fatigue: Ride with the philosophy that you want to bring your horse back to the barn as fresh as when you started.

"Rude" hands: Train yourself to be sympathetic with your hands by visualizing the bit as a razor blade. Imagine it in your mouth, being yanked and pulled.

Unreasonable collection: The development of collection is a slow, methodical process. It cannot be hurried as it takes time to build strength. Also, prolonged periods of collection cause fatigue, so make sure you give your horse lots of breaks to the walk on a loose rein to allow his muscles to relax.

Non-acceptance of the aids: These include the horse being "behind the driving aids" as well as not accepting a contact with your hand.

Put the Horse in Front of the Driving Aids

It's not only just good basic training, but putting your horse in front of *all* of the driving aids—seat, legs, and voice—is a good insurance policy. In fact, you'll note in the chart on page 210 that many resistances, not just rearing, can be fixed by riding your horse *forward* into the contact.

Putting your horse in front of all of the driving aids means that your horse's automatic, conditioned response to seat, leg, and voice, is to move forward eagerly. A horse that "thinks" forward is "hot" off light driving aids. He reacts enthusiastically the moment he feels a push with your seat, a light leg aid, or hears you cluck. (For more on this, see Chapter Six, in *Cross-Train Your Horse*.)

First, educate your horse to respond correctly to each of the driving aids individually. Then, if he's sucking back or actually threatening to rear, you have more ammunition to get a forward reaction by combining two or more of the driving aids. For example, cluck as you close your legs. Or, close your legs as you push with your seat.

Acceptance of the Bit

The second "non-acceptance-of-the-aids" issue concerns your hands—or contact. Often, a horse will react well to the driving aids, but when you touch his mouth, he "hits" your hand and won't happily accept a connection with it. In order to avoid this contact with your hand, some horses back-up, others toss their heads, some come above the bit by putting their heads in the air, some come behind the bit by ducking their heads and putting their chins on their chests, and others threaten to rear.

If you put your hands forward and loosen the reins when your horse tells you he doesn't want to accept your hand, you *reward* him for his behavior. You essentially tell him he's made a choice that works, and that, in the future, he can get you to give up the reins just by threatening to back-up, toss his head, or rear. Instead of dropping the contact, keep a firm, but elastic connection with his mouth, and send him forward into your hands. By doing so, you're telling him that rearing, backing-up, head tossing, coming above the bit, or coming behind the bit are not solutions.

Riding the Rearer

If, in spite of all this training, your horse still rears, here's what you should do to correct this vice. If he just comes slightly off the ground, keep the rein contact to explain to him that rearing won't help him avoid the connection with your hand. However, if your horse rears so high that he's in danger of losing his balance, it's wise to put both your hands and body well forward—even to the point of putting your arms around his neck—so you don't pull him over backward. In both cases, as soon as he comes to the ground after rearing, correct him by kicking vigorously with both legs and use one rein to spin him onto a small circle. Circle several times. Then, straighten him and continue kicking until he goes straight forward. This method works because it makes him go forward, and if he's going forward, he can't rear.

When I was fourteen years old, I used this method very successfully on a horse who was a confirmed rearer. I acquired Dancer from the stable where I took riding lessons because no one wanted to deal with him. He had good reason to start rearing, but that didn't make his behavior any more pleasant—or less dangerous.

When Dancer was a young horse, he had been started very inhumanely. Instead of using a bit, his rider used a piece of baling wire. Poor Dancer's tongue had been torn apart. When it healed, it looked like an hourglass—quite pinched in the middle. Even though his tongue had completely healed and didn't cause him any more physical pain, his memory of those early days was so traumatic that I'm sure he still linked massive emotional pain to any pressure from the bit. Needless to say, Dancer objected very violently to any pressure on his mouth.

I remember the first day I brought him home. My father gave me a leg-up, and the second I touched the saddle Dancer went straight up. I immediately turned him onto a small circle and kicked him vigorously until he was flying around on that circle. I circled several times and then kicked him straight forward out of the circle.

We went along fine for a few minutes and then out of the blue, he slammed on the brakes and reared again. So, I repeated the circling and driving-him-forward method every time he reared, or even threatened to rear. As the week went on, his attempts became less frequent and less dramatic. By the end of the week, he stopped rearing, and he never did it with me again.

I'm not saying that you should want or have to deal with such an extreme vice, but if this approach works so well with a *confirmed* rearer, it's bound to help you out of the occasional tight spot.

To correct rearing, kick vigorously with both legs as soon as your horse comes back to the ground, and use one rein to spin him in a small circle.

Bucking

If your horse bucks from sheer exuberance, he might be a "victim" of overfeeding and/or not enough work. The solution is obvious: Cut his grain ration and increase his exercise.

Then, continue to kick him until he goes straight forward.

If his exuberance stems from having had some time off, or because of a weather change such as a sudden drop in temperature or a gusty wind, longe him for a few minutes before you get on. If you give your horse a chance to get his bucks out of the system before you get on, you'll feel much more confident when you start to ride.

When you are riding, you can usually avert a buck by recognizing the warning signs. In order to buck, your horse slows down, lowers his head, and humps his back, so raise your horse's head as much as you can with a couple of short, sharp tugs on the reins, and then send him forward. If he does start bucking in spite of your efforts, sit upright or a bit behind the vertical. Keep your lower legs forward with your heels down so you're not thrown forward. If that happens, "bridge" the reins so you can brace them against his neck and help regain your balance.

Like many of us, you may be afraid of being thrown off when your horse bucks violently or suddenly. The solution is to attach a "bucking strap" to the front of the saddle. This is a small leather strap that attaches to the D rings on either side of the pommel. When you think your horse might buck, just wrap the fingers of one hand around the strap and pull your seat securely into the saddle so you can stay on without grabbing onto your horse's mouth.

Shying

Most horses shy because they are frightened. Shying is part of their "survival mechanism."

I've found that the best way to work through shying is to not make a big deal about it. Simply distract him by changing his focus. Use your aids to say, "Hey! Think about this!" as you close your legs or vibrate a rein. Or, "Let's do this instead!" as you do a few steps of lengthening and shortening, some quick changes of bend, or a leg-yield.

You can also position your horse's face well away from the scary object. He's a lot less likely to shy at something he can't see. Then, when you're adjacent to whatever is scaring him, soften your reins forward. Softening the contact allows a "claustrophobic" horse to relax—he won't feel as if he's being pinned up against the thing that is terrifying him.

In all cases, be sure you don't add to your horse's anxiety by tensing up and grabbing at the reins. If you do, you're only going to convince him that he was absolutely right to be afraid.

And, since shying stems from fear, the last thing you want to do is punish a horse who is already feeling threatened. You'll only make the problem worse.

A case in point involved a wonderful Trakehner I rode, named Jolicoeur. Jo had a heart of gold but was one of the most timid horses I've ever known.

Jo and I worked out a system to help him cope with the frightening things in life. When he shied , I totally ignored him. I learned that as long as I ignored him, he'd only shy twice. The first shy was usually a pretty dramatic move, and the second, would be much less extreme. He never even looked at the object, the third time by. If I had made a big issue of his shying by kicking him, using the whip, or forcing him to march right up close the first time he saw it, I would have created a huge problem for myself: I'd have to deal with his shying, not only for the remainder of the ride, but probably the next day as well!

I think that the best mind-set to adopt when you ride a horse that shies is to imagine that he's on the alert because he wants to protect both of you. He sees potential danger and warns you by saying, "Did you see that?" By ignoring him, staying relaxed, and of course, never punishing him, you basically say, "Yes. I saw it, but there's no cause for alarm. We're safe. I'll take care of you."

I'm riding Jolicoeur at the US Olympic Festival in Raleigh, North Carolina, 1987.

Bolting

Often, riders describe their horse's resistances by making a value judgment, saying, "My horse was bad." The truth is that most horses don't plan to be "bad," or "good." Often, their behavior is simply a reaction to comfort or discomfort.

For example, the horse that bolts might be looking for an escape from the misery of a pinching saddle, or from a rider who has cranked his neck in so short and tight that his muscles are in spasm. He can only tolerate this discomfort to a point. Then, suddenly he says, "Argh! I can't take it anymore!" and he runs away to get some relief.

Another reason a horse bolts is because, once again, his "survival mechanism" is working the way it's supposed to. Your horse bolts, not because he's bad, but because, in his mind, he's running away from a predator.

Whatever the cause, the bolting horse goes into a "body lock," which makes him difficult to stop. I've found that the simplest method for slowing down and regaining control is to turn your horse in a circle.

Start with a fairly large circle because your horse can lose his balance if he's going really fast and the circle is too small. As he slows down, make the circle progressively smaller. Be sure to sit with your upper body upright, or even better, slightly behind the vertical. *Do not* lean forward. This is like stepping hard on the accelerator! Don't continuously pull on the reins. Your horse will set his jaw against your hands and "numb out" to the pressure in his mouth. Instead, give sharp checks and releases on one, or both reins.

As a last resort, you can use what I call a "pulley" rein. Anchor one hand just in front of your horse's withers. Brace your body weight against that hand, and give several, sharp, upward-and-backward tugs and releases with your other hand.

Emergency Measures

Problem	BOLTING
Causes	Pain; panic or fear; claustrophobia; excess energy; not on aids.
Prevention	Longe if overly fresh.
Short Term Remedy	Break up "body lock" by circling; use pulley rein.
Long Term Resolution	Check tack fit, feed, turnout, and exercise; Arrange vet check to examine for pain.
Problem	BUCKING
Causes	Pain; excess energy; overfed/underworked; "cold back"; cinchiness; unbalanced rider; rider's leg drawn too far back on a ticklish horse; using whip on hindquarters.
Prevention	Longe; circle so horse concentrates on his balance; ride forward.
Short Term Remedy	Go briskly forward; raise horse's head; keep your upper body upright or lean back.
Long Term Resolution	Evaluate feed and exercise; longe a cold-backed horse; use elastic girth on "cinchy" horse and tighten it gradually; keep horse "in front of leg"; ride forward; don't use leg or whip too far back on hindquarters.

Problem	RELUCTANCE TO GO FORWARD—SUCKING BACK
Causes	Tension; pain; horse is "behind the leg"; incorrect collection (cranked-in and "lifted" in front by rider's hands); indiscriminate or overuse of leg.
Prevention	Put horse "in front of leg"; breathe; do quick transitions within the gait; use your eyes to look forward to the spot you want to ride toward.
Short Term Remedy	Soften hands; ride forward from seat and legs.
Long Term Resolution	Scrutinize tack fit (saddle and bit); ask vet to check back, hocks, mouth; teach horse to be "hot" off light, leg aids; collect horse by engaging hindquarters, *not* by using hands; train yourself to relax (*progressive relaxation; autogenics; sonic meditation; scanning; deep relaxation; belly breathing; plus/minus signs; clicking the pen; and squeezing the sponge*).
Problem	REARING
Causes	Fright; tension; frustration from confusion or fatigue; pain; lack of "acceptance of aids"; a harsh bit; rough hands; too much collection asked for too soon; "behind the leg."
Prevention	Train horse to be in front of the driving aids.
Short Term Remedy	Maintain "elastic" contact; circle, and send horse forward by kicking vigorously.
Long Term Resolution	Teach horse to be "hot" off all the driving aids; make sure horse is sufficiently strong, supple, prepared, and rested to do what you're asking.
Problem	SHYING
Causes	Fear; inattention; tension; excess energy; insecurity; poor vision.
Prevention	Longe if overly fresh.
Short Term Remedy	Stay relaxed; do not punish; ignore shying; turn horse's head away from what he's afraid of; do frequent transitions to get horse to concentrate on you.
Long Term Resolution	Evaluate feed, turnout, and exercise; check vision; increase turnout time; build confidence by schooling in a firm, consistent manner and by exposing horse to different situations.

Essentials of Coping with Fear

- Courage is not the absence of fear. Being courageous means being afraid but taking a risk or doing a job *in spite of* your fear.
- If you focus on your fear, your subconscious mind will move you toward it.
- Break your pattern of fear by *thought stopping*. Yell out a word like, "Stop!" or "Relax!"
- Once you've done some *thought stopping*, use *visualization* and *self-talk* to replace negative thoughts with positive ones.
- Banish fear by having an *attitude of gratitude*.
- Rather than interpreting fear as a signal to retreat, think of it as a *green light* to move ahead.
- Turn your, "*What if's?*" into "So *what if's?*" Then follow that question up with an, "*I can handle it.*"
- Most of what we're afraid of never comes to pass. Keep fear under control by learning how to *stay in the moment*.
- *Bargain with your fear* so you don't spend your entire ride obsessing about it.
- The better you can communicate with your horse, the safer he'll be. Teach him to stop, go, slow down, and turn with the lightest of aids.
- Set the stage for safety: Learn some strategies to deal with bolting, bucking, sucking back, rearing, and shying.

A re you a pessimistic person? Do you always see the glass half empty rather than half full? I think we become pessimistic out of a need to protect ourselves. We reason that if we expect the worst, we won't be hurt or disappointed when it happens. And, if the worst doesn't happen, it's just a bonus.

The pessimist drives herself "nuts" with worry. She assumes when her horse comes up slightly lame that it is a serious problem like a torn suspensory ligament. If her horse gets a little colicky, he's a candidate for surgery. If he tosses his head when being ridden, she's sure she's ruining him. If she's scheduled to be one of the first competitors in a class, she's concerned that the judge isn't "warmed-up" enough yet to give good scores. Or, if she's scheduled to ride toward the end of the class, she's concerned that the judge will be tired and cranky!

Pessimism is a character trait you really need to change. If you see the dark side of every situation, you're going to have a hard time enjoying yourself. Remember that attitude is a choice. You can choose to be optimistic as easily as you can choose to be pessimistic. Some time ago, I received a letter from a three-day event rider who learned this lesson the hard way. She wrote:

"I am competing at the Intermediate and Advanced levels. In October, my husband and I, along with three horses, went to a horse trials near San Francisco. Our trip started out poorly when we stopped at a fast food restaurant for breakfast, and our wheelbarrow was stolen out of our pickup truck. Later, we got a flat tire, and discovered that our spare was flat, too. Then, I got a call from my groom who

Attitude is a choice.
Dress appropriately.

said she had an emergency and wouldn't be able to come help me. The final straw was when I got to the event and saw that two of my stalls were flooded, and the third had a pole in the middle of it!

"I soon adopted an attitude, 'What bad thing is going to happen next?' And, of course, with that pessimistic attitude, I got exactly what I expected. The show ended up being a total disaster. I forgot my dressage test twice. One horse got eliminated at the water obstacle. And, I crashed through several jumps in show jumping.

"That was a good lesson for me. After that show, I realized I needed an *attitude adjustment*. I made a conscious decision to change my thinking at my next horse trials a month later. Whenever I got nervous at the competition, I clung to an enthusiastic, optimistic mindset by saying, 'I can't wait to get out on course so everyone can see how great my horse is.'

"Well, it was the best event I ever competed in. I won two championships and was fourth on my third horse."

If you want another lesson in the power of optimism, take a page from a little boy's story I read in *Chicken Soup for the Soul*. He was overheard talking to himself as he strode through his backyard, baseball cap in place and toting ball and bat. "I'm the greatest baseball player in the world," he said proudly. Then, he tossed the ball in the air, swung and missed. Undaunted, he picked up the ball, threw it into the air, and said to himself, "I'm the greatest player ever!" He swung at the ball again, and again he missed. He paused a moment to examine bat and ball carefully. Then, once again he threw the ball into the air and said, "I'm the greatest baseball player who ever lived." He swung the bat hard and again missed the ball.

"Wow!" he exclaimed. "What a pitcher!"

Pessimism to Optimism

- Attitude is a choice. Decide to see the glass half full rather than half empty.

- If you're feeling pessimistic, give yourself an *attitude adjustment.*

- No matter what happens, be the greatest rider that ever was!

Appendix

Reprinted from *Cross-Train Your Horse: Simple Dressage for Every Horse, Every Sport,* by Jane Savoie.

Longeing Equipment

I'm assuming that your horse is not an unbroken youngster and has already been under saddle. Prepare him for his longeing session by first tacking him up with a bridle and a saddle. Remove the bridle's reins or tie them up out of the way by twisting one rein around the other and feeding the throatlatch through one of the loops. Tie up the stirrups by winding the leathers around them and feeding the free end of the leather through the loop (figs. 1 to 3).

Basic equipment for longeing includes a longeing cavesson, two side reins, a longe line and a whip. It's important for the cavesson to fit securely so it doesn't move around and perhaps rub against his eye. Place the cavesson on his head and secure the noseband first. Then fasten the cavesson's throatlatch. A halter is a poor substitute for a cavesson, but if you opt to use one over the bridle, be sure to adjust it very snugly so it doesn't twist or slide around and rub your horse's outside eye. Never attach your longe line to the bit because it could hurt the bars of your horse's mouth.

I also recommend using gloves because it can be pretty painful to have a fresh horse pull a nylon or web longe line through your hands. Without gloves, rope burn might force you to let go so that your horse ends up running around with a

Fig. 1 To prevent the rein from hanging down, twist one rein around the other and feed the throatlatch of the bridle through one of the loops before you fasten it.

Fig. 2 Place the longeing cavesson on your horse's head and secure the noseband first. The cavesson should fit snugly so it doesn't shift and rub your horse's eye.

thirty-foot longe line trailing along behind him. If that happens, he might panic and bolt or perhaps get himself tangled up in the line. At best, he'll scare himself, and at worst, he could be badly hurt.

I also like to put boots or bandages on my horse's legs to protect them from damage if they hit each other.

Both the longe line and the longe whip should be long—at least thirty feet long for the line and a minimum of twelve feet, including the lash, for the whip. The line should be long enough so that your horse can make a fairly large circle, yet not so long that you can't influence him with your body, voice and whip. The circle you should make with most horses is twenty meters in diameter (approximately sixty feet).

Hold the longe line in your leading hand (that is the left hand if the horse is tracking to the left), with the slack layered back and forth across the palm of your hand. Never wind the slack around your hand, because it can be dangerous if your horse decides to take off (fig. 4).

Hold the longe whip in the other hand. Ideally, the whip needs to be long enough for you to stand in the center of your circle and, if necessary, reach the horse's barrel with the lash. I've been known to put "extenders" like shoe laces on the end of whips to make the lash longer. You see, in order for a circle to be a good gymnastic shape in terms of teaching the horse something about balance, it must be round. You may say, "well a circle is always round," but it's nearly impossible to make a round circle if you're walking along with the horse because your whip is too short. You need to be able to stand almost still in one spot and just pivot around your leading leg. For example, when your horse is circling to the left, you pivot around your left leg, which remains in the same spot. Stand with your feet apart and your knees slightly bent so that you can absorb any sudden movement.

Side reins, which attach from the girth to the rings of the bit above the reins, can be made of all leather, leather and elastic, or with a round rubber doughnut insert. I personally prefer all leather because some horses feel the "give" in the elastic and test the contact by pulling or snatching at the reins. I don't want them to learn how to do this on the longe because I certainly don't want them doing it when I ride. The side reins with the rubber doughnut are a good compromise because they provide some give without being too "stretchy."

When I'm ready to use the side reins, I'll attach them to the back billet strap on the saddle. I don't place them around both billets or around the entire

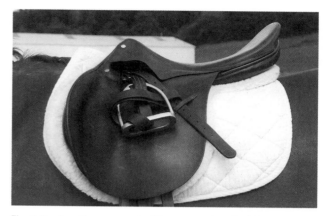

Fig. 3 Tie the stirrups up out of the way so they don't bang against your horse's sides.

Fig. 4 Safety first. Layer the excess longe line back and forth across your hand. Never wind it around your hand or let it drag on the ground where you could get it wrapped around your foot.

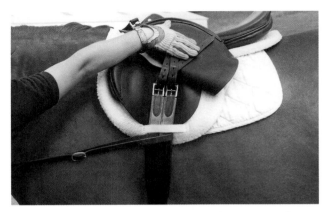

Fig. 5 Place the side reins around the back billet to prevent them from slipping down too low on the girth.

Fig. 6 Make sure that the side reins are the same length. They should be short enough to establish a light contact with your horse's mouth but long enough so that he doesn't feel confined.

girth because I don't want them to slip down too low. As far as the height of the side reins is concerned, a good rule of thumb is that they should be placed at the height of the rider's knee (fig. 5).

However, I always lead the horse away from and back to the stable with the side reins unhooked. I do this prior to work because the horse's body is stiff and cold from standing in the stall. I don't want him suddenly to feel restricted or surprised by the side reins while walking out of the barn, because he could run backward or rear and hurt himself seriously. I unhook them after work as a reward.

When I'm in the arena ready to work, I attach the side reins loosely. I adjust them long enough so the horse doesn't feel stifled, restricted, or crammed into a frame, but short enough so that there is a light contact with his mouth and so that his outside shoulder doesn't pop out of the line of the circle (fig. 6).

I almost always keep the two side reins the same length. Some people like to have the inside side rein a couple of inches shorter because they believe this helps the horse bend to the inside of the circle. The danger here is that the hindquarters might swing to the outside of the circle in order to avoid the increased bend caused by the shorter inside side rein. If you discover that your horse's tendency is to escape to the outside with his hindquarters, it's best to keep the side reins the same length.

Notes

CHAPTER 1 1. Ziglar, Zig. *See You at the Top* . Pelican Publishing Company, 1978, pp.160-167

          2. Robbins, Anthony. *Get the Edge*, audiotape series. Robbins Research International Inc, 2001

          3. Robbins, Anthony. *The Time of Your Life*, audiotape series. Robbins Research International Inc, 1998

          4. Loving, Nancy. *Go the Distance.* North Pomfret: Trafalgar Square Publishing, 1997, pp.98-100

          5. Pulos, Dr. Lee. *The Power of Visualization*, audiotape series. Nightingale Conant Corporation

          6. Robbins, Anthony. *Personal Power—Classic Edition*, audiotape series. Robbins Research International Inc, 1996

          7. *Get the Edge*

CHAPTER 2 1. Maltz, M.D., Maxwell. *Psychocybernetics.* New York: Pocket Books, 1960, p.2

          2. *See You at the Top*, p.185

          3. Loehr, James. Ed. D., *The New Toughness Training for Sport.* New York: Penguin Group, 1995, p.23

          4. Baum, Kenneth.*The Mental Edge.* New York: Berkley Publishing Group, 1999, p.49

          5. Robbins, Anthony. *Unleash the Power Within*, seminar. December 2001

CHAPTER 3 1. *Get the Edge*

          2. *Unleash the Power Within*

CHAPTER 5 1. Matthews, Andrew. *Being Happy.* Media Masters Pte Ltd, 1999, p.8

          2. Carlson, Richard. *Everything I Eat Makes Me Thin.* New York: Bantam Books, 1991, p.12

          3. Canfield, Jack and Hansen, Mark Victor. *Dare to Win.* New York: Berkley Books, 1996, p.20

          4. Psychocybernetics, p.18

          5. Helmstetter, Shad. *What to Say When You Talk to Yourself.* New York: Pocket Books, 1987, p.59

          6. *Being Happy*, p.57

          7. Donovan, Jim. *Handbook to a Happier Life.* Bovan Publishing Group, 1998, p.24

CHAPTER 6   1. Savoie, Jane, with Sloane, Stephen. *To Dance with Your Horse.* Dressage Today, September, 1999
2. *Unleash the Power Within*
3. Ibid

CHAPTER 7   1. *The Power of Visualization*
2. Ibid
3. Trudeau, Kevin. *Mega Memory.* Nightingale Conant Corporation, 1991
4. *The Mental Edge*, pp.14-15
5. *See You at the Top*, p.193

CHAPTER 9   1. *The Power of Visualization*
2. Schulte, Barbra. *Mentally Tough Riding*, audiotape series. LGE Sport Science Inc, 1996

CHAPTER 11   1. *Everything I Eat Makes Me Thin*, pp.24-5
2. *The Power of Visualization*
3. Ibid
4. Robbins, Anthony. *Date With Destiny*, seminar. February 2002
5. *The Power of Visualization*

CHAPTER 13   1. *The Power of Visualization*
2. Ibid

CHAPTER 15   1. *See You at the Top,* pp.202-203
2. Ibid, p.231
3. Ibid, p.228

CHAPTER 17   1. *Unleash the Power Within*

CHAPTER 19   1. *The Power of Visualization*
2. Ibid
3. Ibid
4. Ibid

CHAPTER 20   1. *The New Toughness Training for Sport.* pp.168-9

CHAPTER 21   1. Jeffers, Susan. *Feel the Fear and Do It Anyway.* New York: Ballantine Books, 1987, pp.27-9
2. Jeffers, Susan. *Feel the Fear...And Beyond.* New York: Ballantine Publishing Group, 1998, p.42
3. Tellington-Jones, Linda. *Improve Your Horse's Well-Being.* North Pomfret: Trafalgar Square Publishing, 1999, p.8

Selected Bibliography

Bassett, Lucinda. *From Panic to Power.* New York: Harper Collins Publishers, 1995.

Bassett, Lucinda. *Life Without Limits.* New York: Harper Collins Publishers, 2001.

Baum, Kenneth. *The Mental Edge.* New York: The Berkley Publishing Group, 1999.

Bristol, Claude. *The Magic of Believing.* New York: Pocket Books, 1948.

Bush, Karen. *The Problem Horse.* New York: Howell Book House, 1992.

Canfield, Jack and Hansen, Mark Victor. *Dare to Win.* New York: Berkley Books, 1996.

Carlson, Richard. *Everything I Eat Makes Me Thin.* New York: Bantam Books, 1991.

Donovan, Jim. *Handbook to a Happier Life.* Bovan Publishing Group, 1998.

Edgette, Janet. *Heads Up!* New York: Doubleday, 1996.

Garfield, Charles. *Peak Performance.* New York: Warner Books, 1984.

Gross, Darwin. *Power of Imagination.* US, 1998.

Helmstetter, Shad. *The Self-Talk Solution.* New York: Pocket Books, 1987.

Helmstetter, Shad. *What to Say When You Talk to Yourself.* New York: Pocket Books, 1987.

Jeffers, Susan. *Feel the Fear...And Beyond.* New York: Ballantine Publishing Group, 1998.

Jeffers, Susan. *Feel the Fear and Do It Anyway.* New York: Ballantine Books, 1987.

Keller, Jeff. *Attitude is Everything,* Florida: INTI Publishing and Resource Books, Inc., 1999.

Loehr, James. Ed. D., *The New Toughness Training for Sport.* New York: Penguin Group, 1995.

Loving, Nancy. *Go the Distance.* North Pomfret: Trafalgar Square Publishing, 1997.

Maltz, M.D., Maxwell. *Psychocybernetics.* New York: Pocket Books, 1960.

Maltz, Maxwell. *Psycho-Cybernetic Principles for Creative Living.* New York: Pocket Books, 1974.

Martorano, Joseph and Kildahl, John. *Beyond Negative Thinking.* New York: Avon Books, 1989.

Matthews, Andrew. *Being Happy.* Media Masters Pty Ltd, 1999.

Maxwell, John. *The Winning Attitude,* Tennessee: Thomas Nelson Publishers, 1993.

Murphy, Joseph. *The Power of Your Subconscious Mind.* New York: Bantam Books, 1963.

Murphy, Shane. *The Achievement Zone.* New York: Berkley Books, 1996.

Peale, Norman Vincent. *Positive Imaging*. New York: Ballantine Books, 1982.

Peale, Norman Vincent. *The Amazing Results of Positive Thinking*. New York: Fawcett World Library, 1959.

Peale, Norman Vincent. *The Positive Principle Today*. New York: Fawcett Books, 1976.

Peale, Norman Vincent. *The Power of Positive Living*. New York: Ballantine Books, 1990.

Peale, Norman Vincent. *The Power of Positive Thinking*. New York: Fawcett Books, 1952.

Pulos, Dr. Lee. *The Power of Visualization*, audiotape series. Nightingale Conant Corporation.

Robbins, Anthony. *Awaken the Giant Within*. New York: Simon and Schuster, 1991.

Robbins, Anthony. *Date With Destiny*, seminar. February 2002.

Robbins, Anthony. *Get the Edge*, audiotape series. Robbins Research International Inc, 2001.

Robbins, Anthony. *Personal Power—Classic Edition*, audiotape series.

Robbins, Anthony. *The Time of Your Life*, audiotape series. Robbins Research International Inc, 1998.

Robbins, Anthony. *Unleash the Power Within*, seminar. December 2001.

Robbins, Anthony. *Unlimited Power.* New York: Simon and Schuster, 1986.

Schuller, Robert. *Move Ahead with Possibility Thinking*. New York: Spire Books, 1978.

Schuller, Robert. *You Can Become the Person You Want To Be.* New Jersey: Spire Books, 1973.

Schulte, Barbra. *Mentally Tough Riding*, audiotape series. LGE Sport Science Inc, 1996.

Schwartz, David. *The Magic of Getting What You Want*. New York: Berkley Books, 1983.

Schwartz, David. *The Magic of Self-Direction*. New York: Parker Publishing Company, Inc., 1965.

Schwartz, David. *The Magic of Thinking Big*. New York: Cornerstone Library, 1959.

Tellington-Jones, Linda. *Improve Your Horse's Well-Being*. North Pomfret: Trafalgar Square Publishing, 1999.

Teague, Juanell. *The Zig Ziglar Difference*. New York: Berkley Books, 1999.

Thomas, Paul. *Advanced Psycho-Cybernetics*. New York: Perigee Books, 1985.

Trudeau, Kevin. *Mega Memory*. Nightingale Conant Corporation, 1991.

Waitley, Denis. *Being the Best*. New York: Pocket Books, 1987.

Waitley, Denis. *Seeds of Greatness*. New York: Pocket Books, 1983.

Waitley, Denis. *The Double Win*. New York: Berkley Books, 1985.

Waitley, Denis. *The Psychology of Winning.* New York: Berkley Books, 1979.

Waitley, Denis. *Timing is Everything,* Pocket Books, New York, 1992.

Ziglar, Zig. *Over the Top*. Tennessee: Thomas Nelson Publishers, 1994.

Ziglar, Zig. *Top Performance*. New York: Berkley Books, 1986.

Ziglar, Zig. *See You at the Top*. Pelican Publishing Company, 1978.

Photo Credits

Index

Page numbers in *italic* indicate illustrations.